**LARGE
PRINT**

Calm
Dot-to-Dot

LARGE PRINT
Calm
Dot-to-Dot

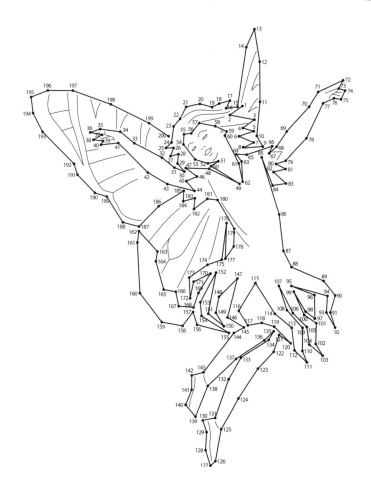

David Woodroffe

SIRIUS

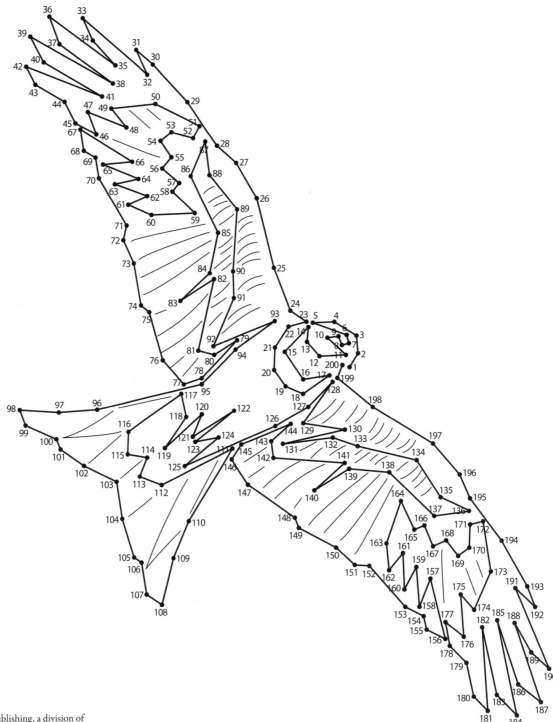

SIRIUS

This edition published in 2022 by Sirius Publishing, a division of
Arcturus Publishing Limited,
26/27 Bickels Yard, 151–153 Bermondsey Street,
London SE1 3HA

ISBN: 978-1-3988-2036-4
CH010355NT
Supplier 29, Date 0522, PI 00001706

Printed in China

INTRODUCTION

When everyday life is becoming a little too much and you need something to take your mind off things, doing a puzzle or two can be a simple and effective way to unwind and recharge.

Within these pages, you will find a wonderful selection of images to complete – from fantastical creatures to works of art, famous people and everyday objects.

All you have to do is pick up a pen or pencil and find dot number one and then follow the rest of the dots until you reach the final number. As you focus on joining them together, you'll discover that you put your cares to one side while you create your selected image.

So, why not find a comfortable chair, get yourself a relaxing drink or even a little sweet treat, and get going, and above all, have fun!

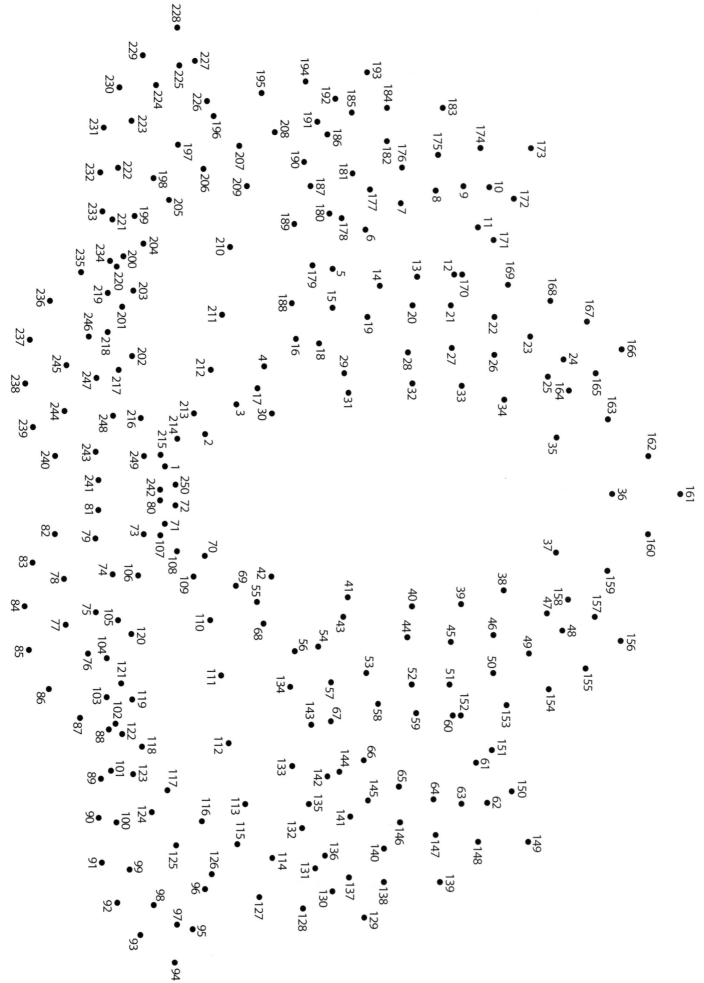

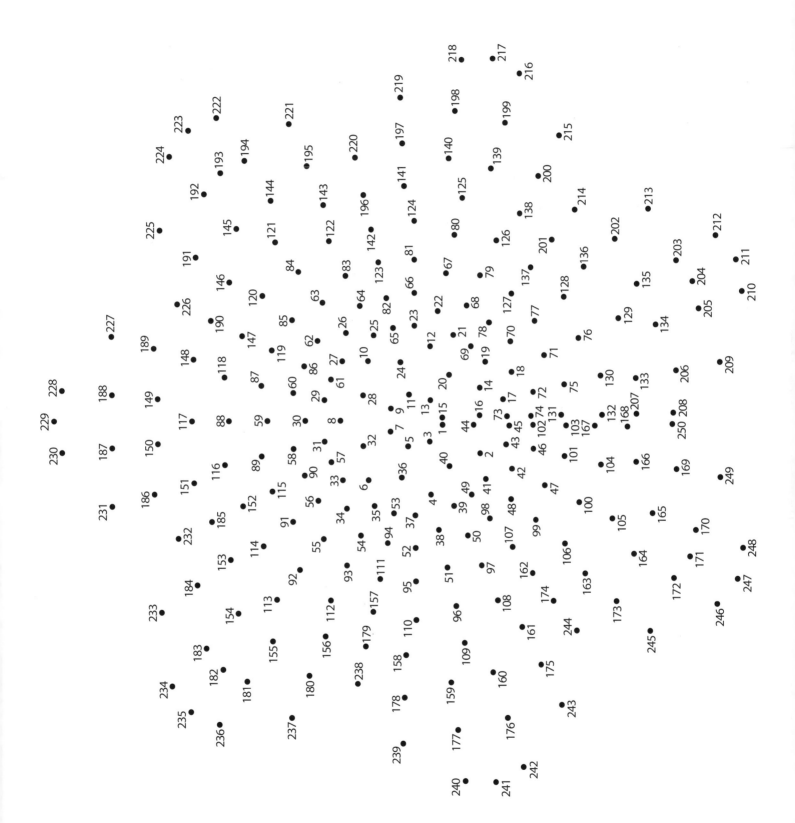

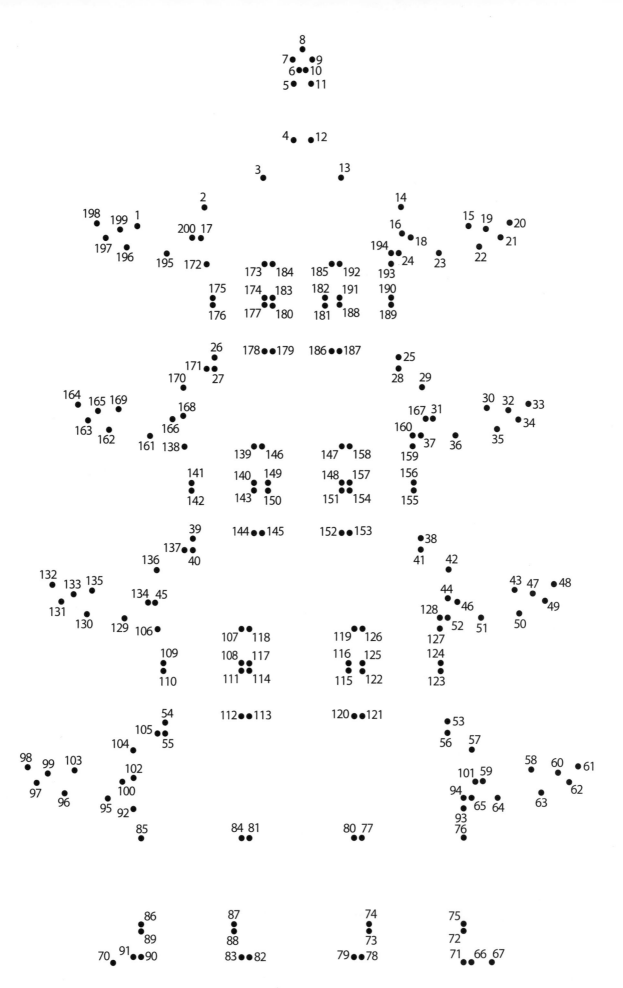

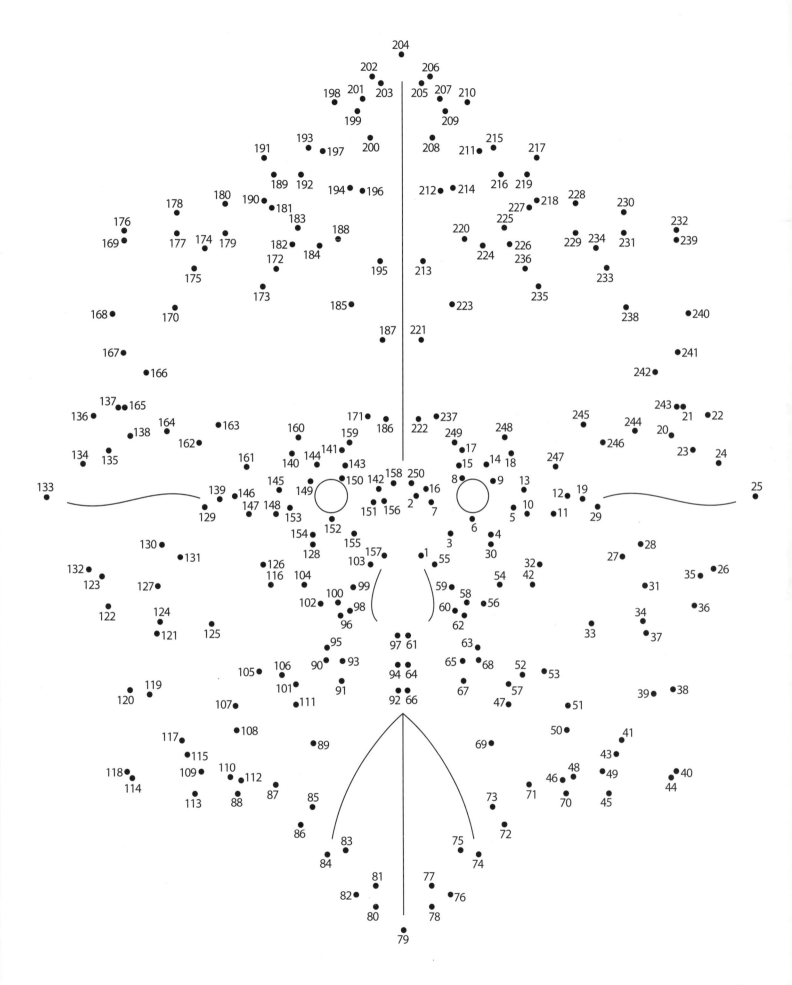

10

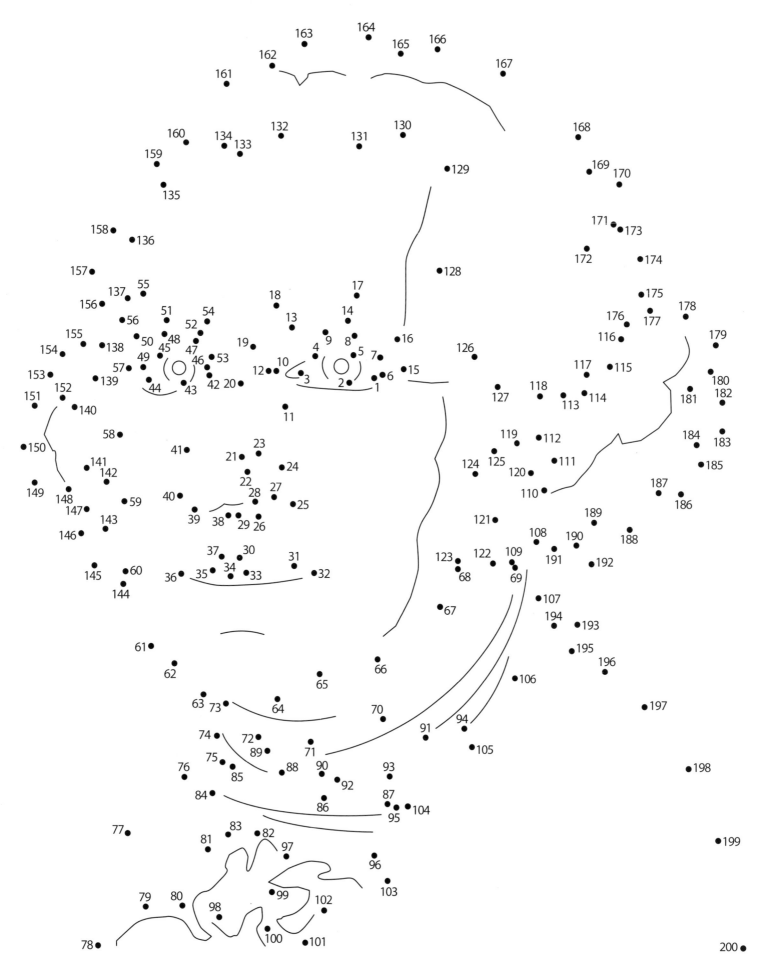

1
22● ●20 ●18 ●16 ●14 ●12 ●10 ●8 ●6 ●4 2
●

●21 19● ●17 15● ●13 11● ●9 7● ●5 ●3
●24 26● ●28 30● ●32 34● ●36 38● ●40 ●42

23● ●25 ●27 ●29 ●31 ●33 ●35 ●37 ●39 ●41 ●43
63● ●61 ●59 ●57 ●55 ●53 ●51 ●49 ●47 ●45

●62 60● ●58 56● ●54 52● ●50 48● ●46 ●44
●65 67● ●69 71● ●73 75● ●77 79● ●81 ●83

64● ●66 ●68 ●70 ●72 ●74 ●76 ●78 ●80 ●82 ●84
104● ●102 ●100 ●98 ●96 ●94 ●92 ●90 ●88 ●86

●103 101● ●99 97● ●95 93● ●91 89● ●87 ●85
●106 108● ●110 112● ●114 116● ●118 120● ●122 ●124

105● ●107 ●109 ●111 ●113 ●115 ●117 ●119 ●121 ●123 ●125
145● ●143 ●141 ●139 ●137 ●135 ●133 ●131 ●129 ●127

●144 142● ●140 138● ●136 134● ●132 130● ●128 ●126
●147 149● ●151 153● ●155 157● ●159 161● ●163 ●165

146● ●148 ●150 ●152 ●154 ●156 ●158 ●160 ●162 ●164 ●166
186● ●184 ●182 ●180 ●178 ●176 ●174 ●172 ●170 ●168

●185 183● ●181 179● ●177 175● ●173 171● ●169 ●167
●188 190● ●192 194● ●196 198● ●200 202● ●204 ●206

187● ●189 ●191 ●193 ●195 ●197 ●199 ●201 ●203 ●205 ●207
227● ●225 ●223 ●221 ●219 ●217 ●215 ●213 ●211 ●209

●226 224● ●222 220● ●218 216● ●214 212● ●210 ●208
●229 231● ●233 235● ●237 239● ●241 243● ●245 ●247

●248
228● ●230 ●232 ●234 ●236 ●238 ●240 ●242 ●244 ●246 ●
● 249
250

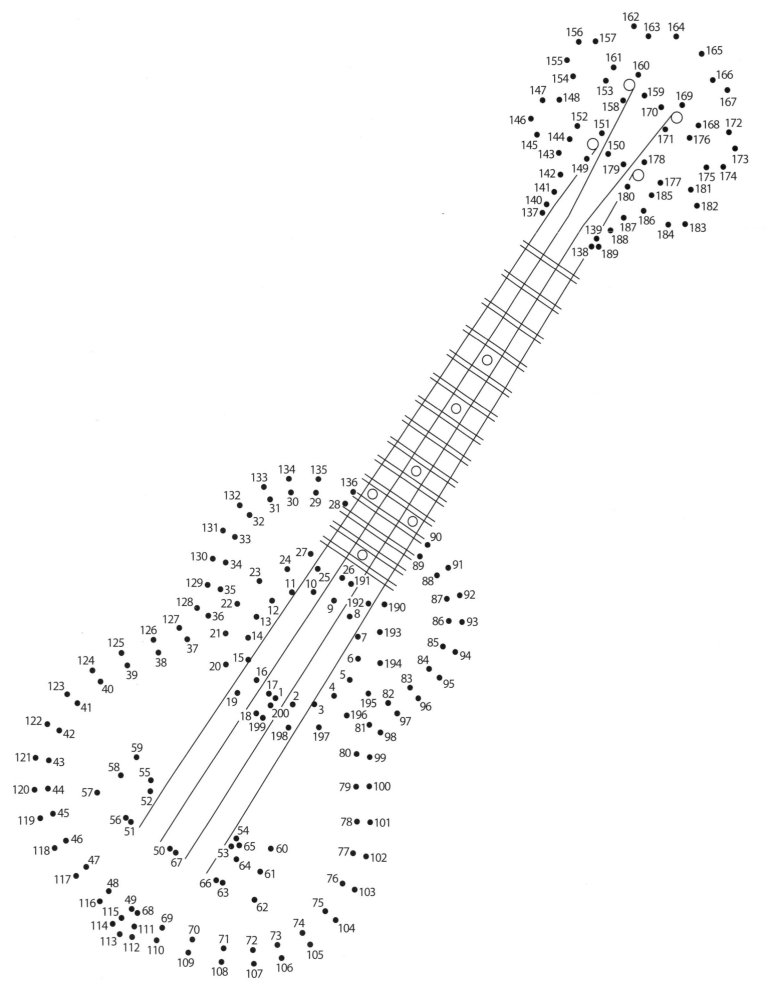

13

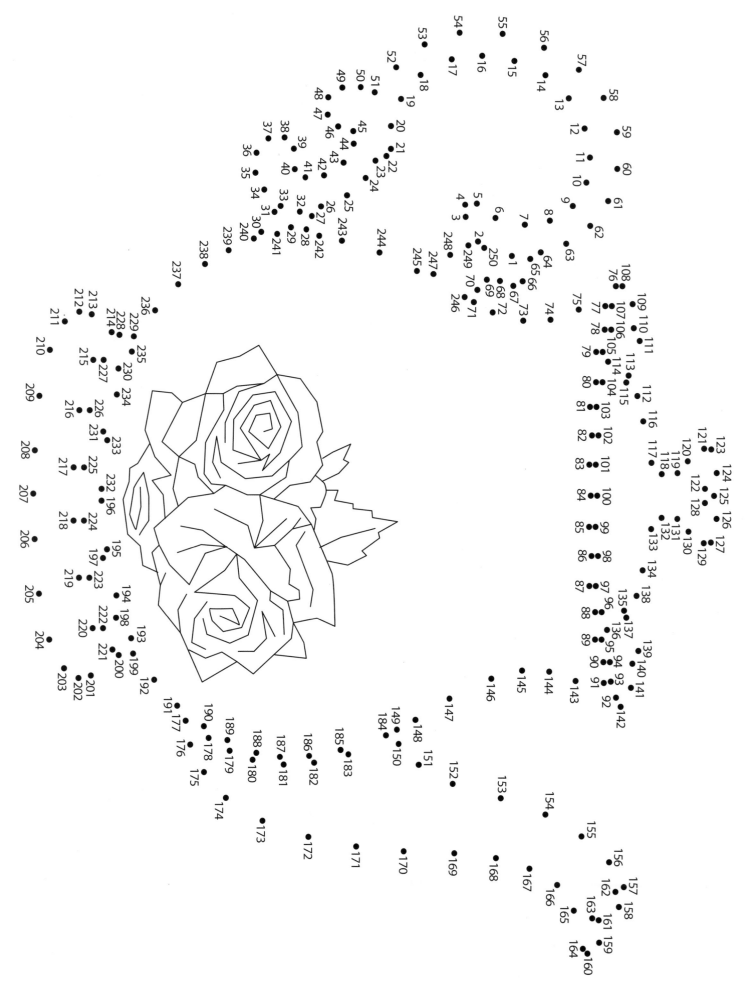

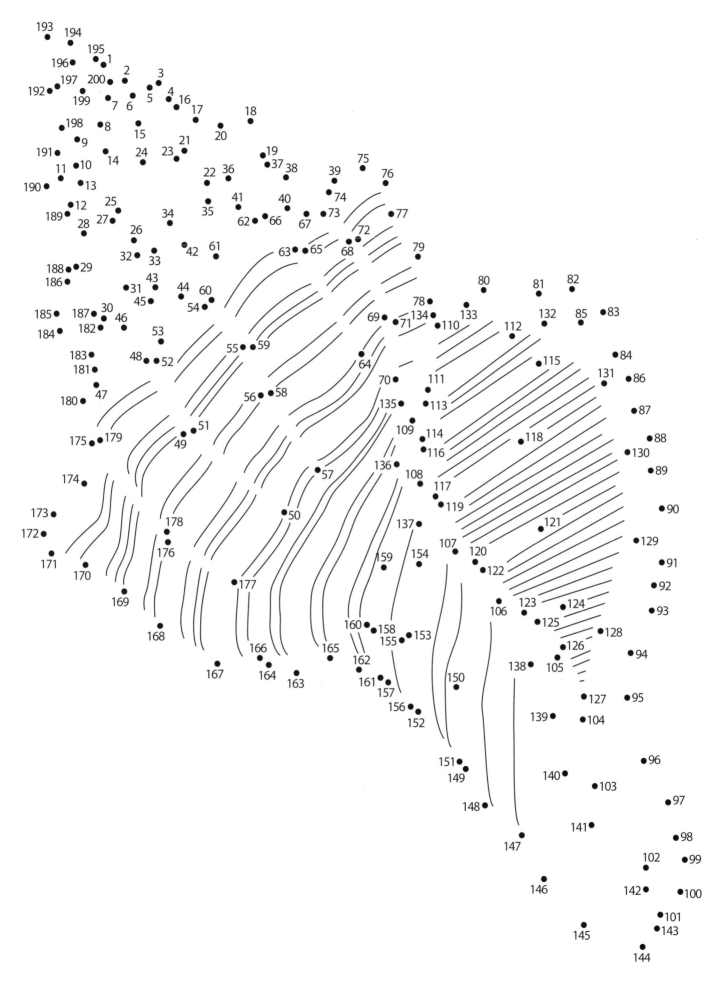

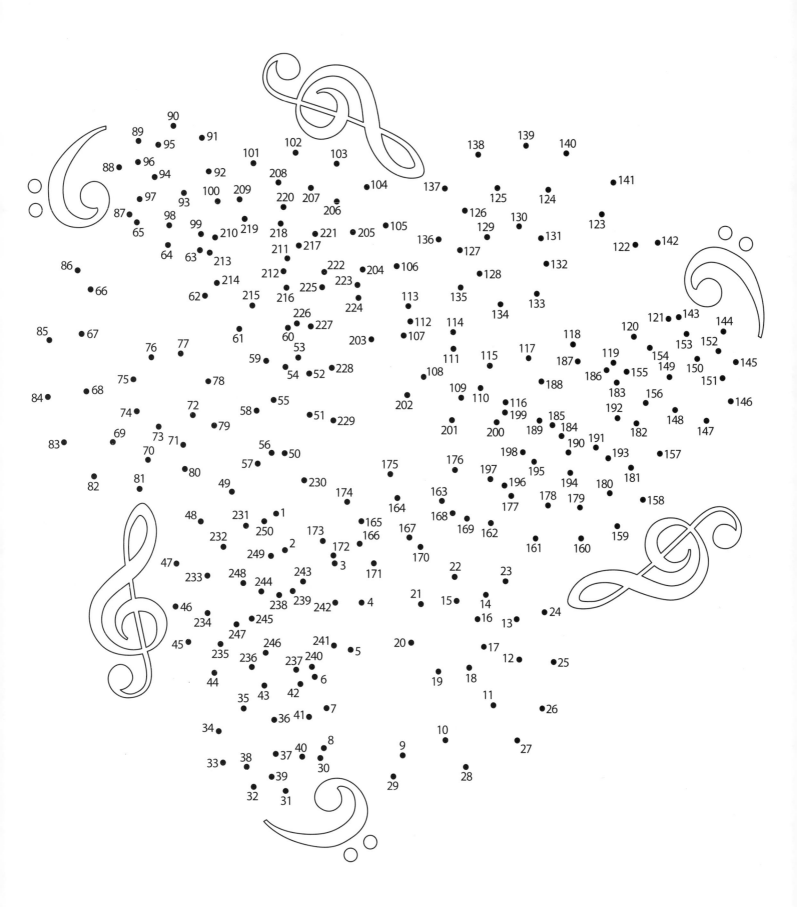

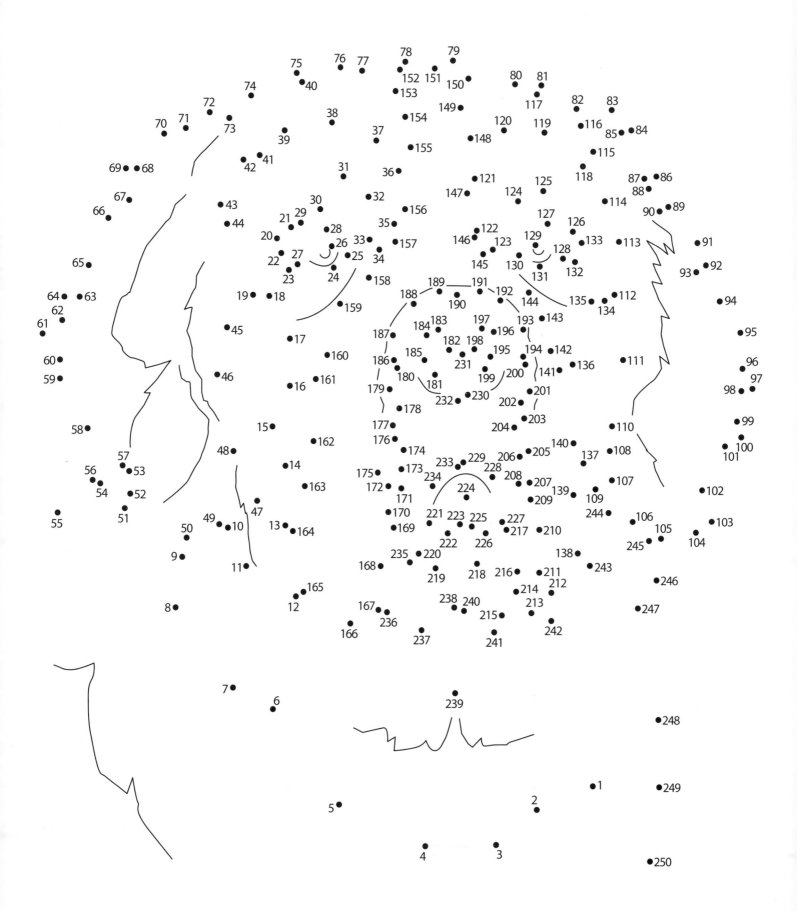

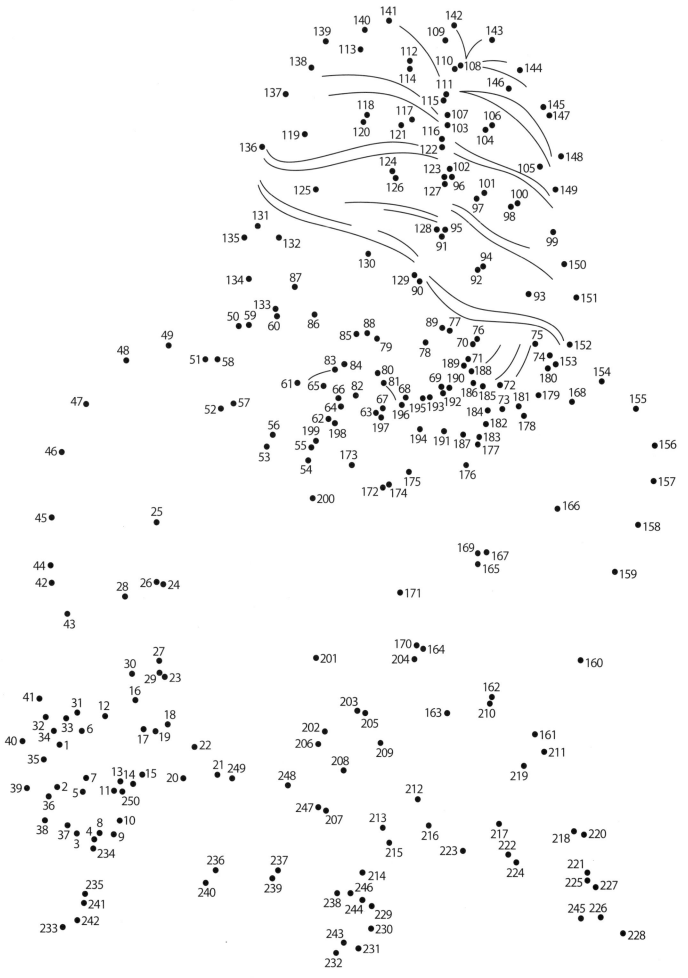

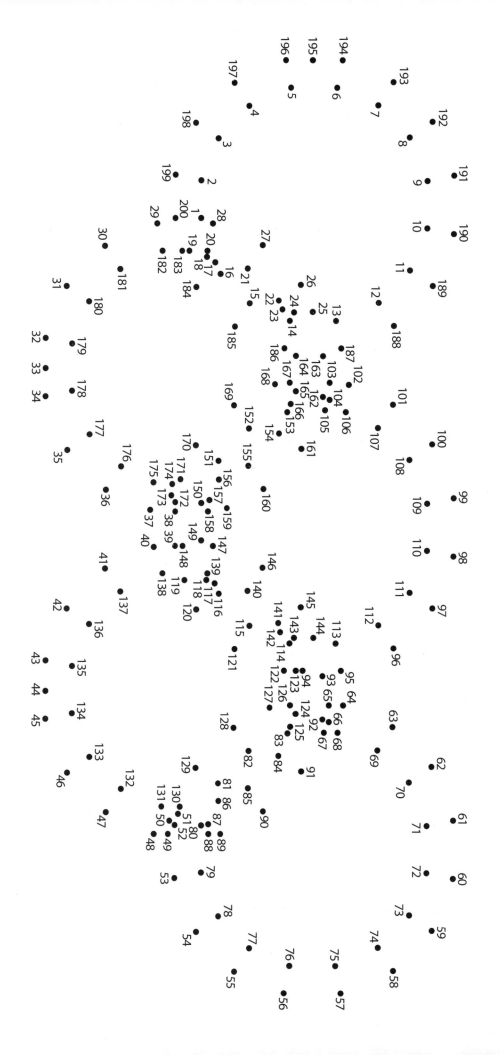

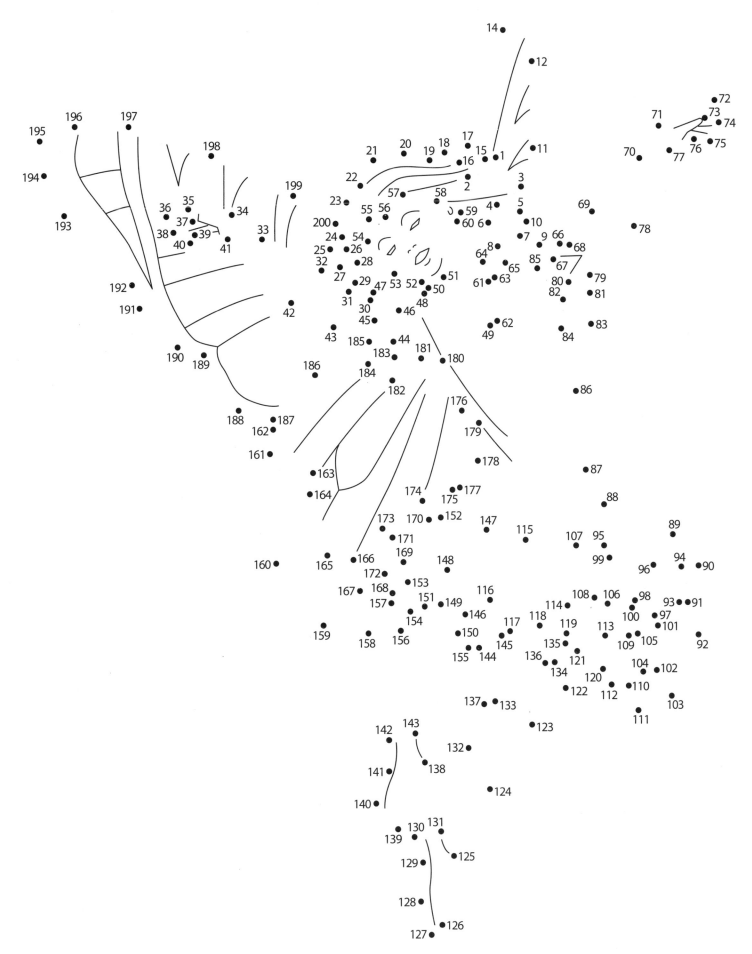

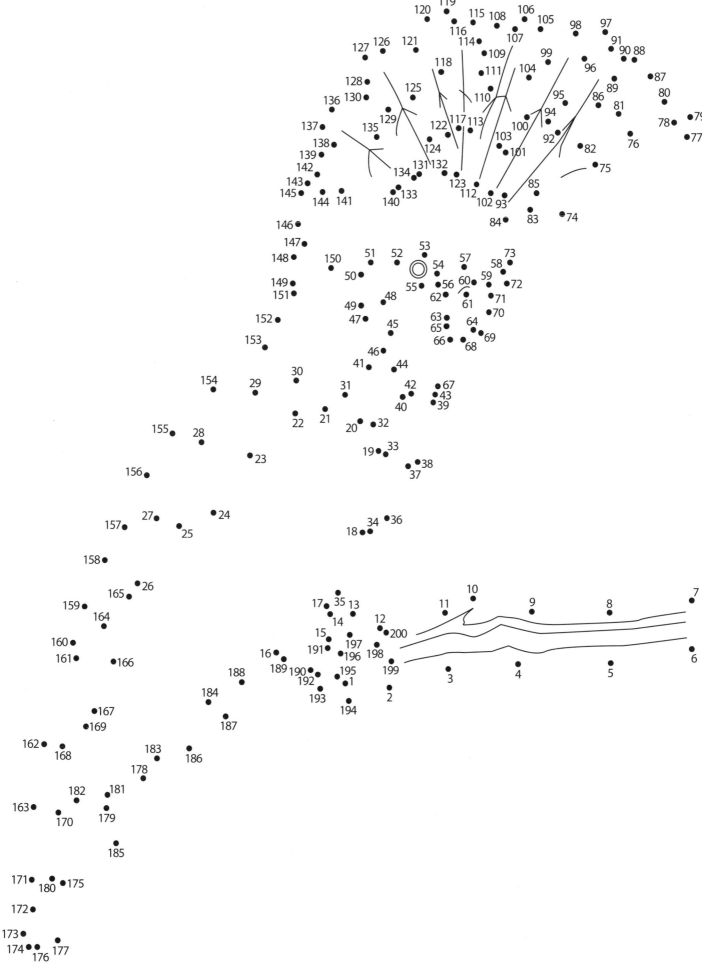

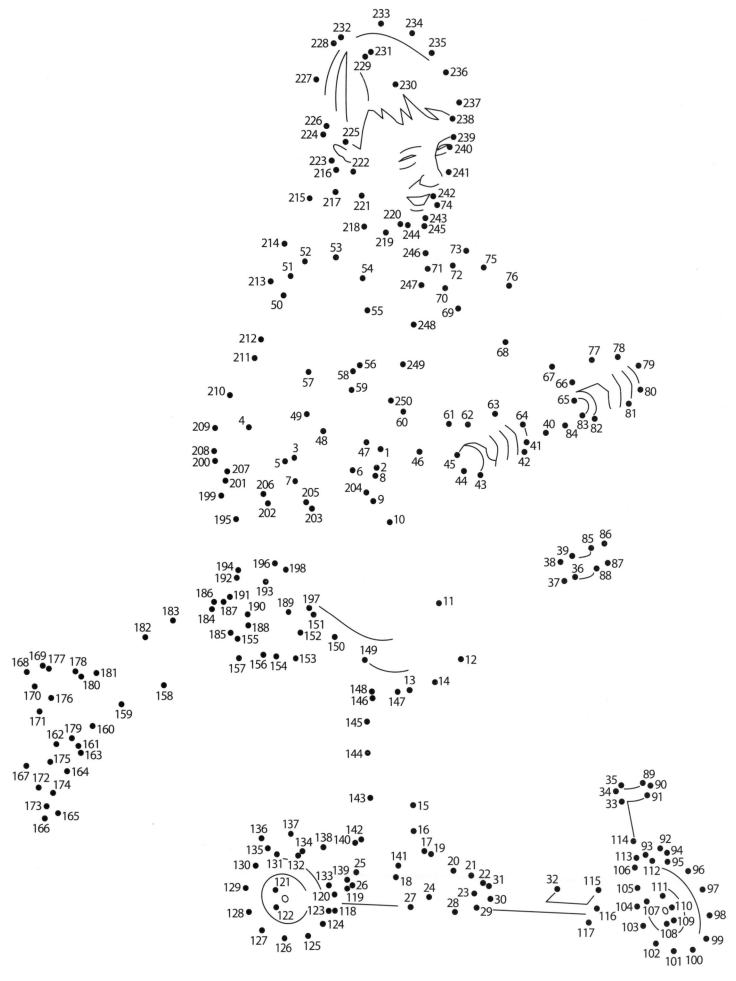

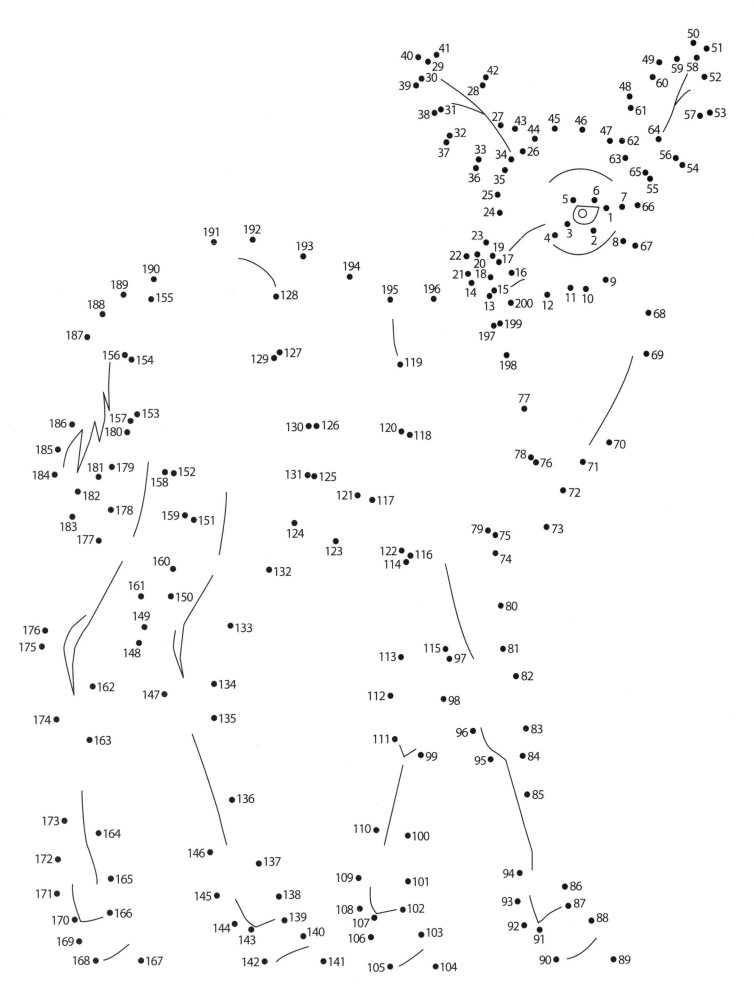

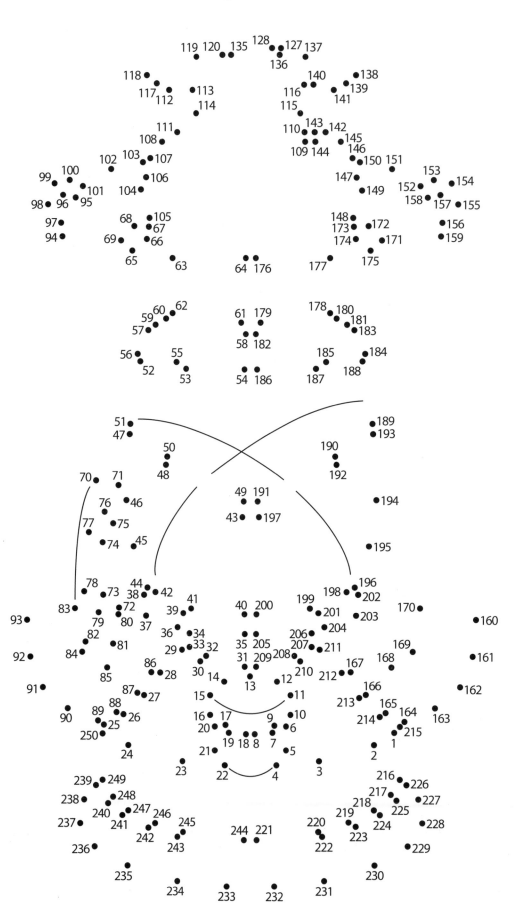

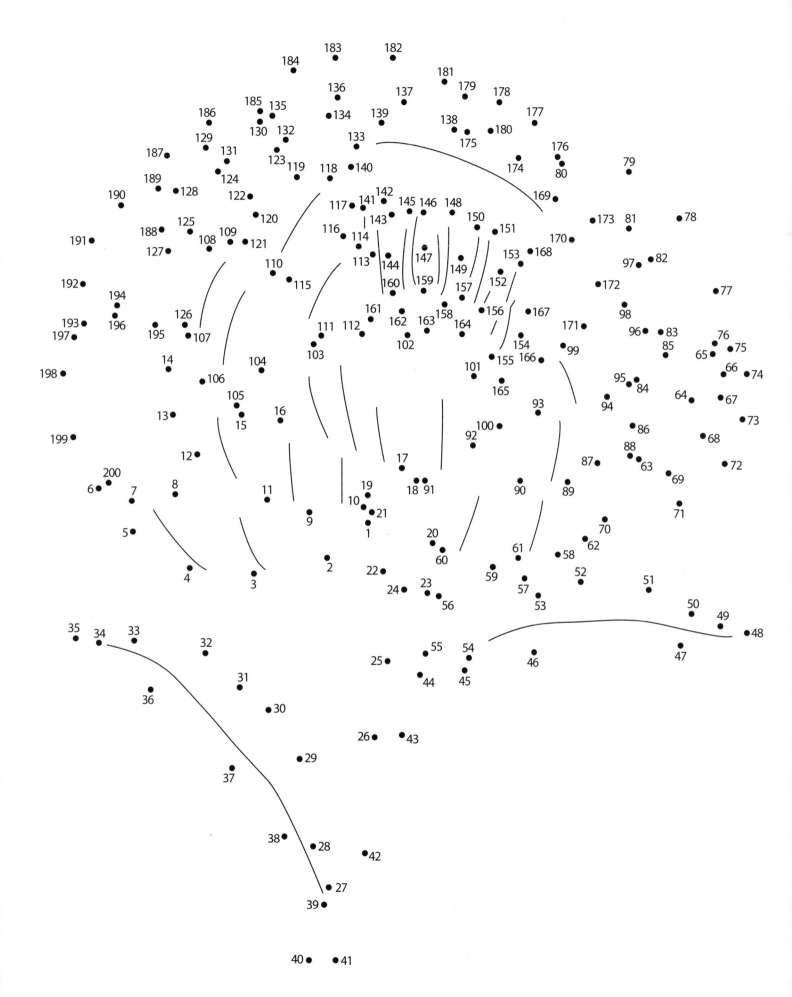

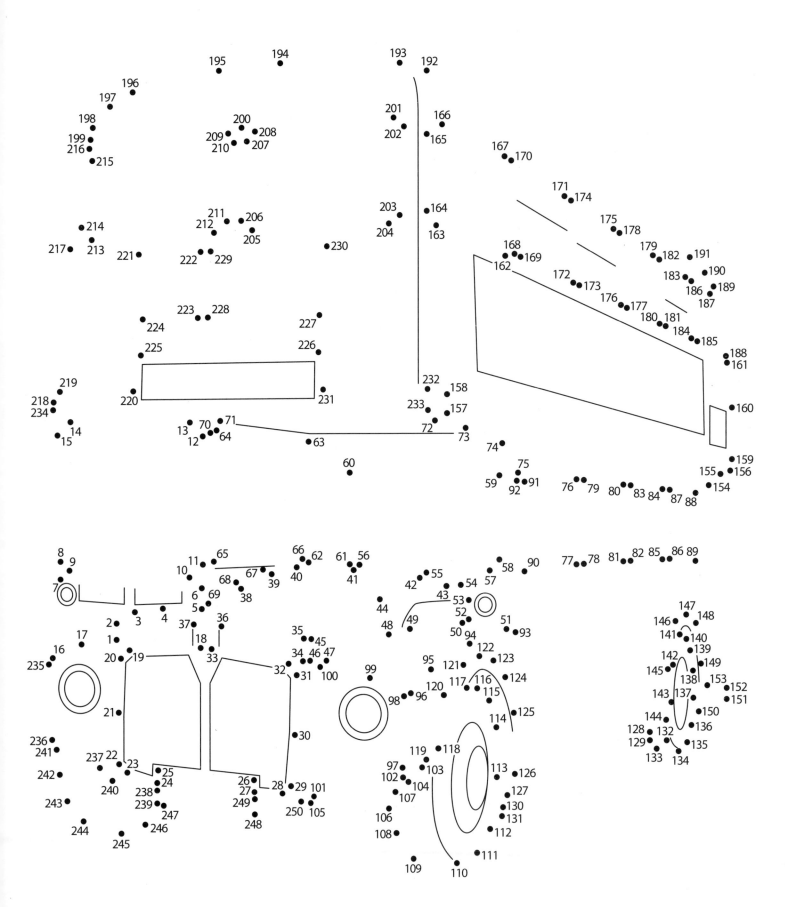

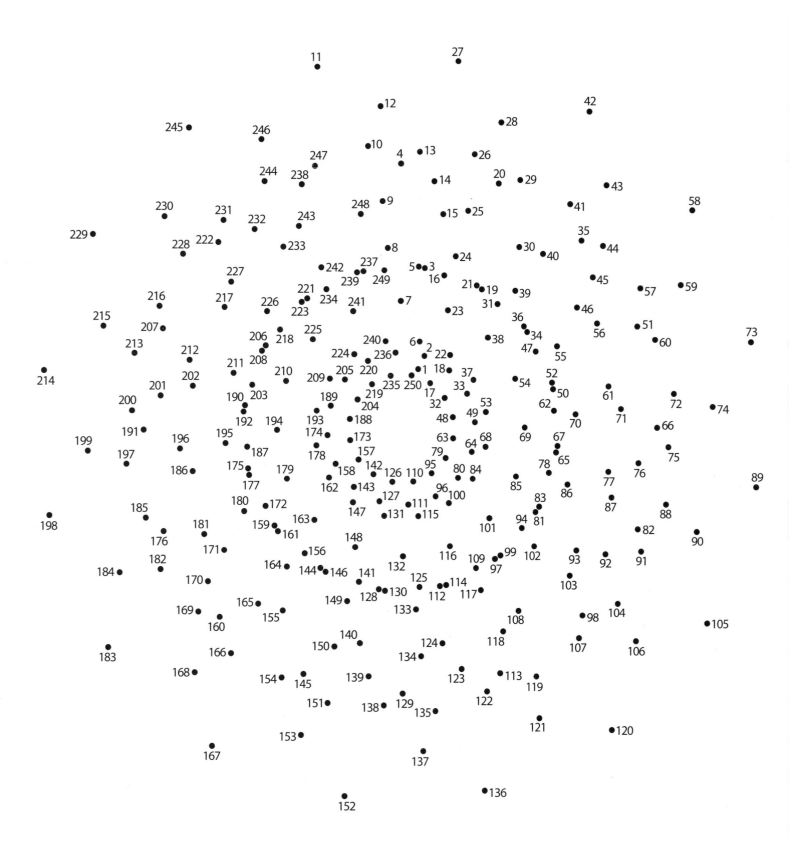

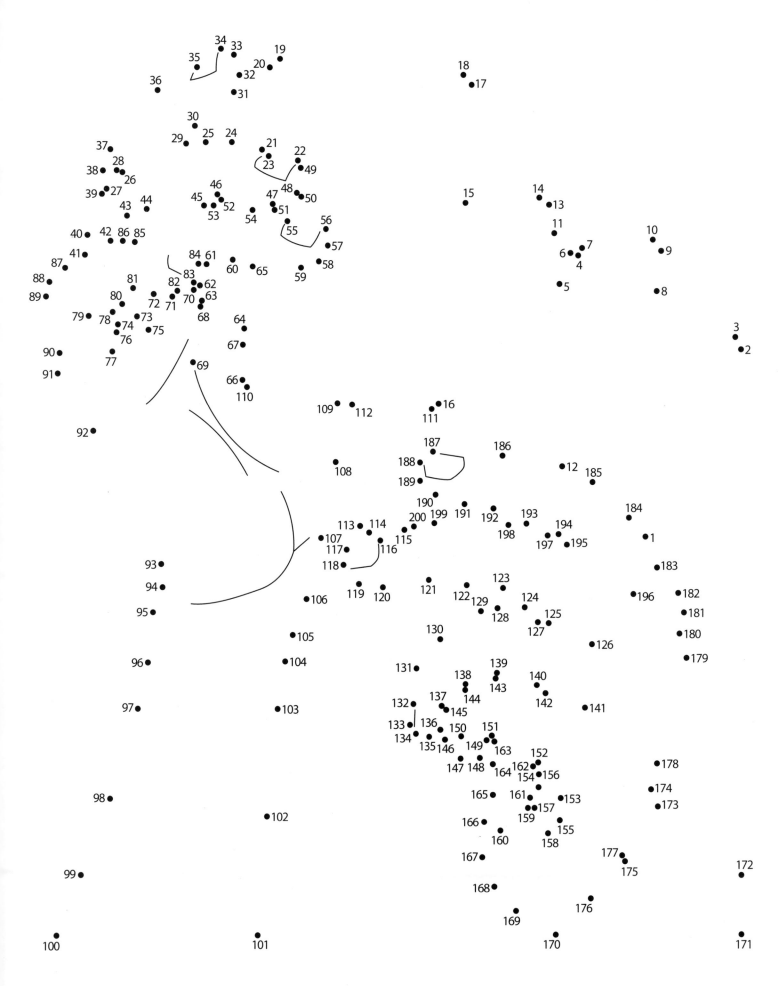

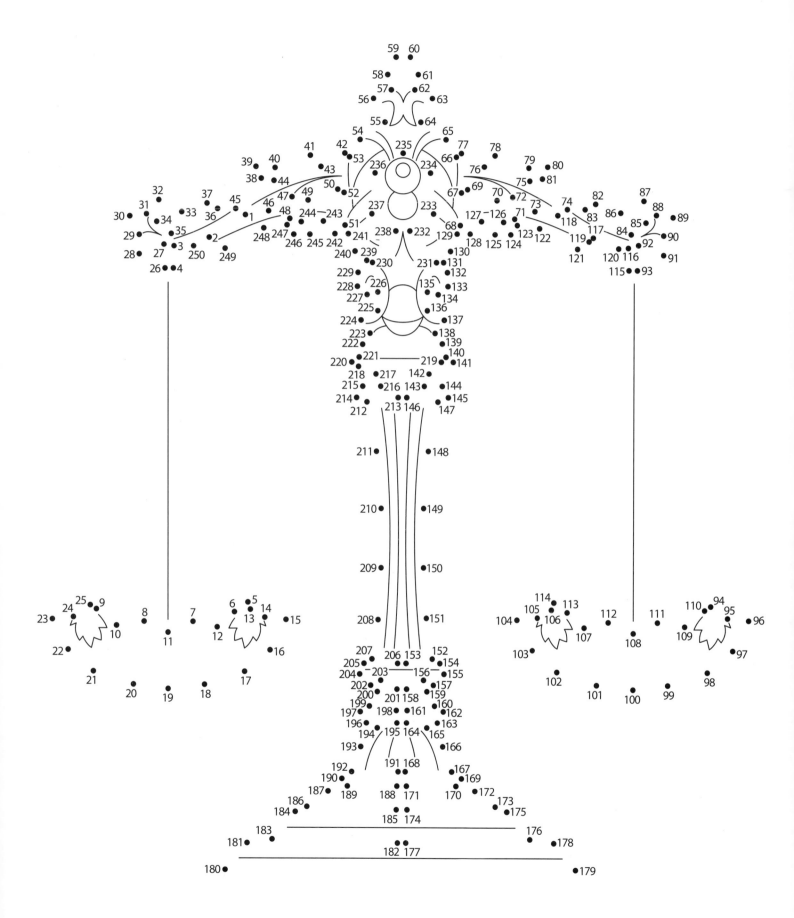

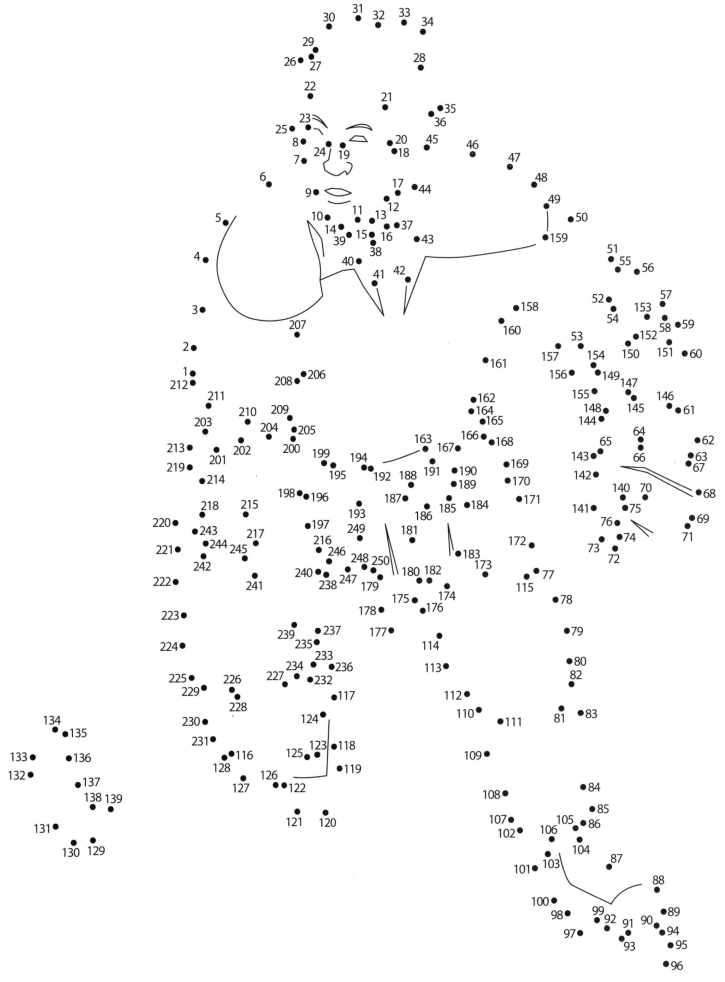

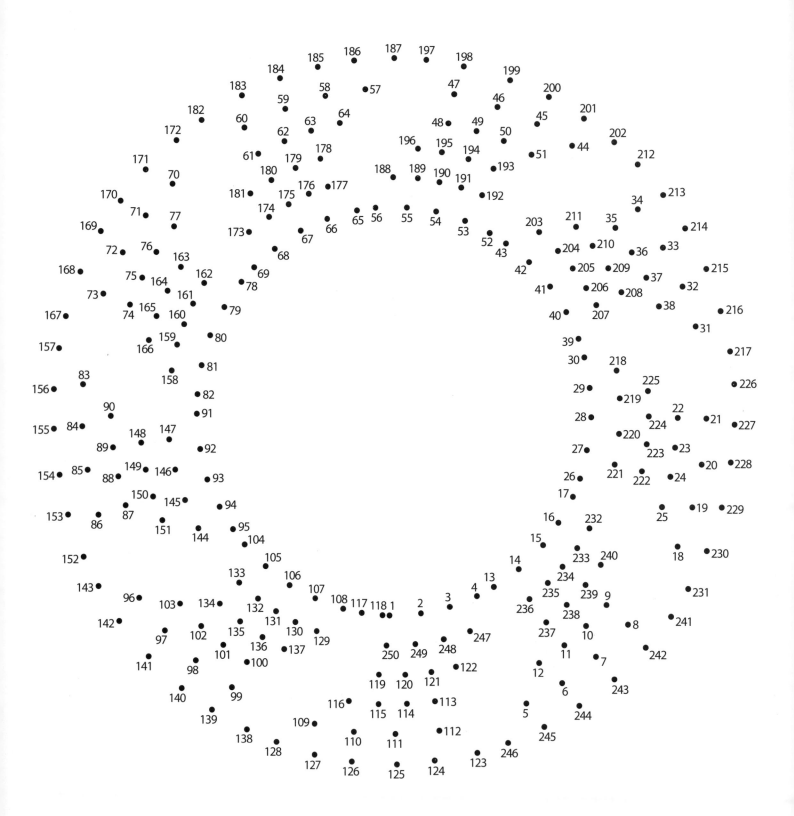

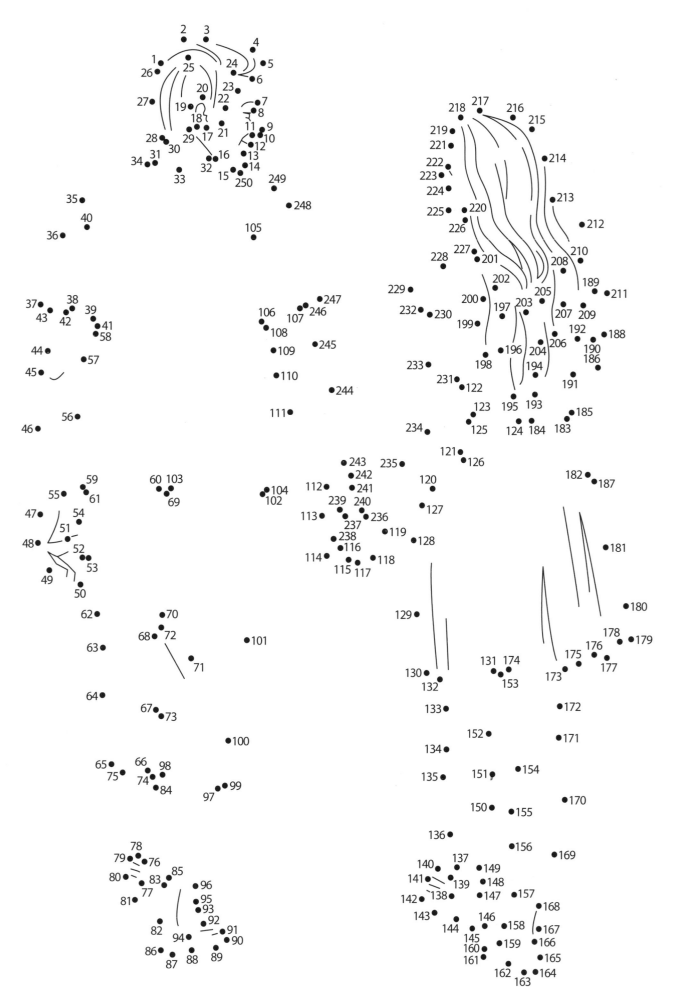

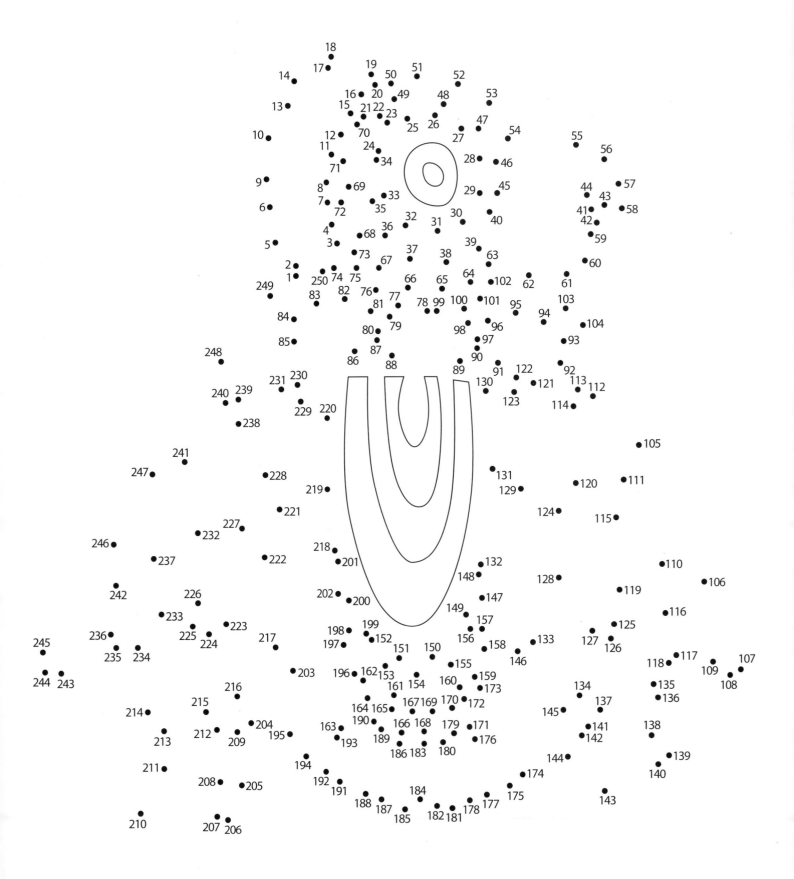

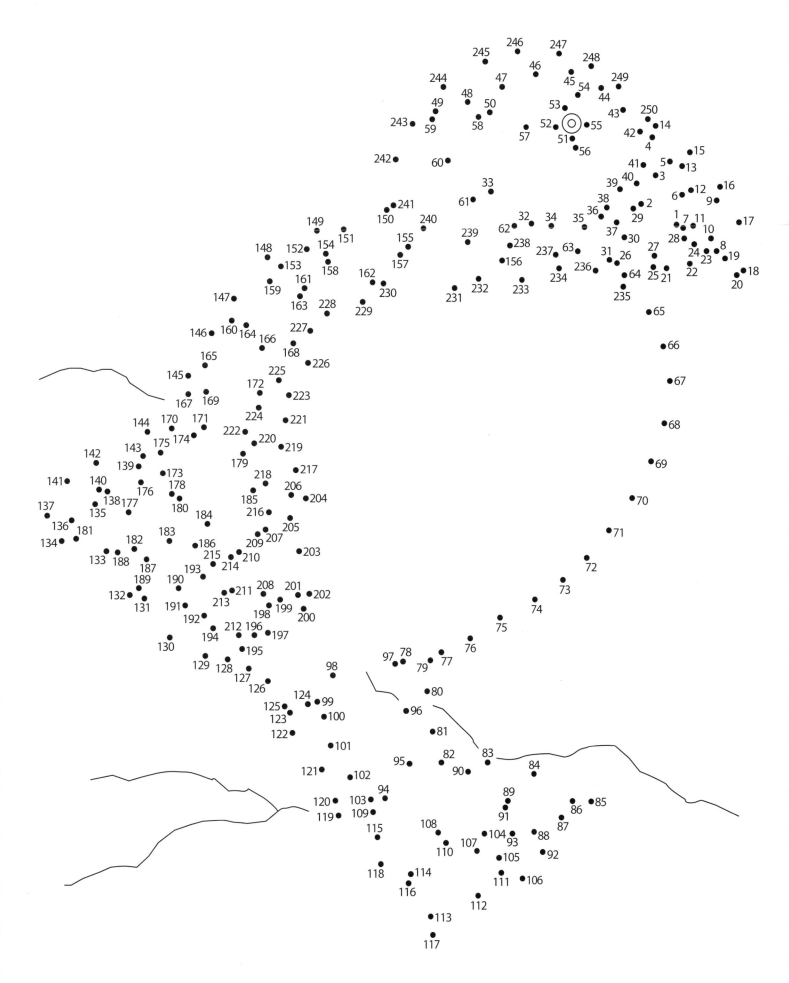

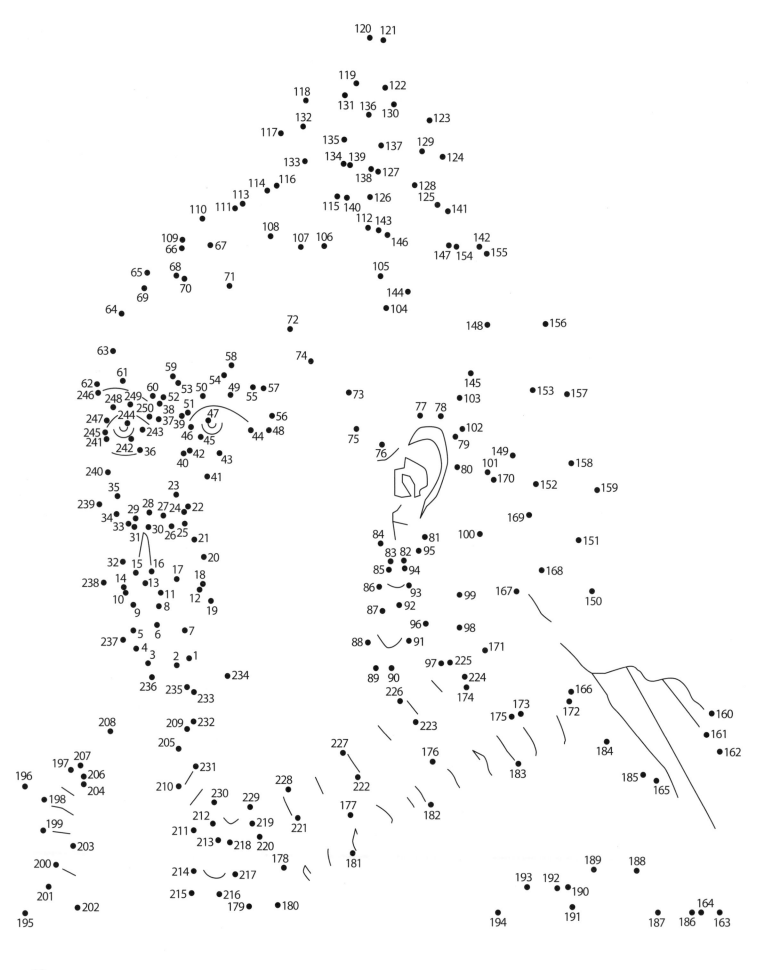

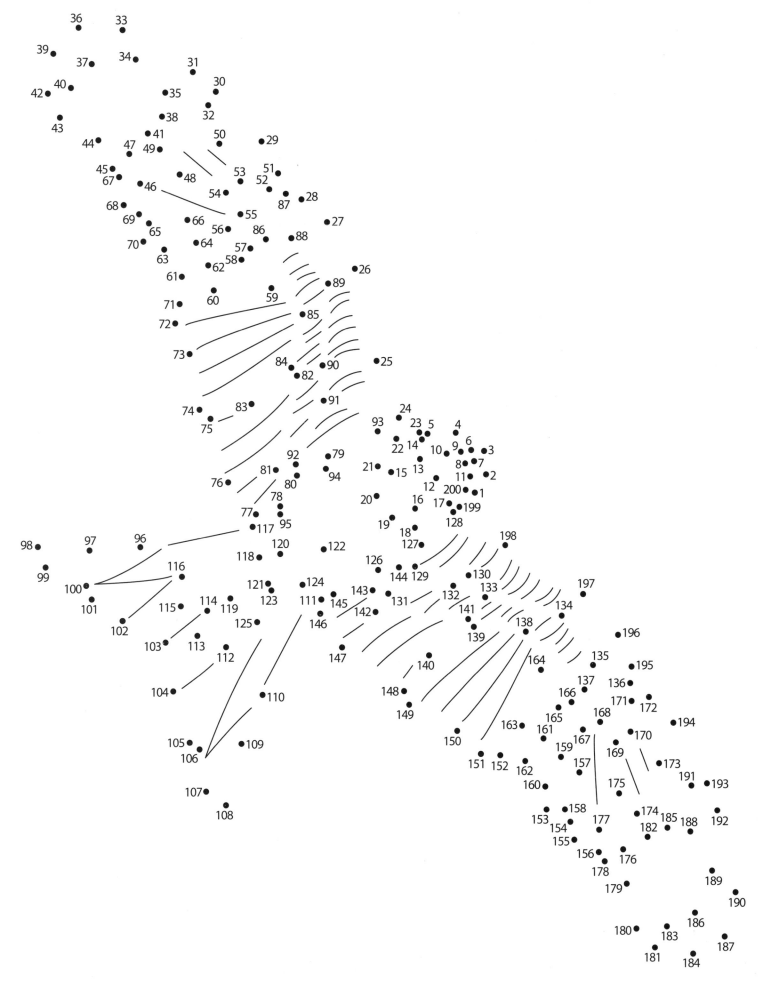

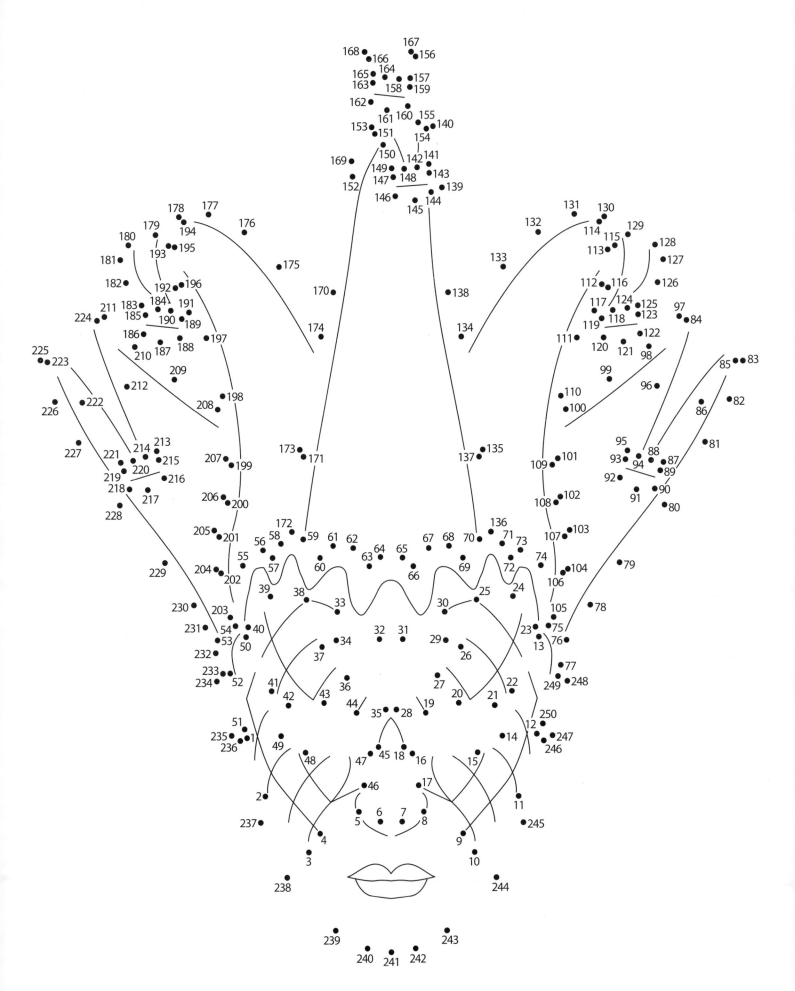

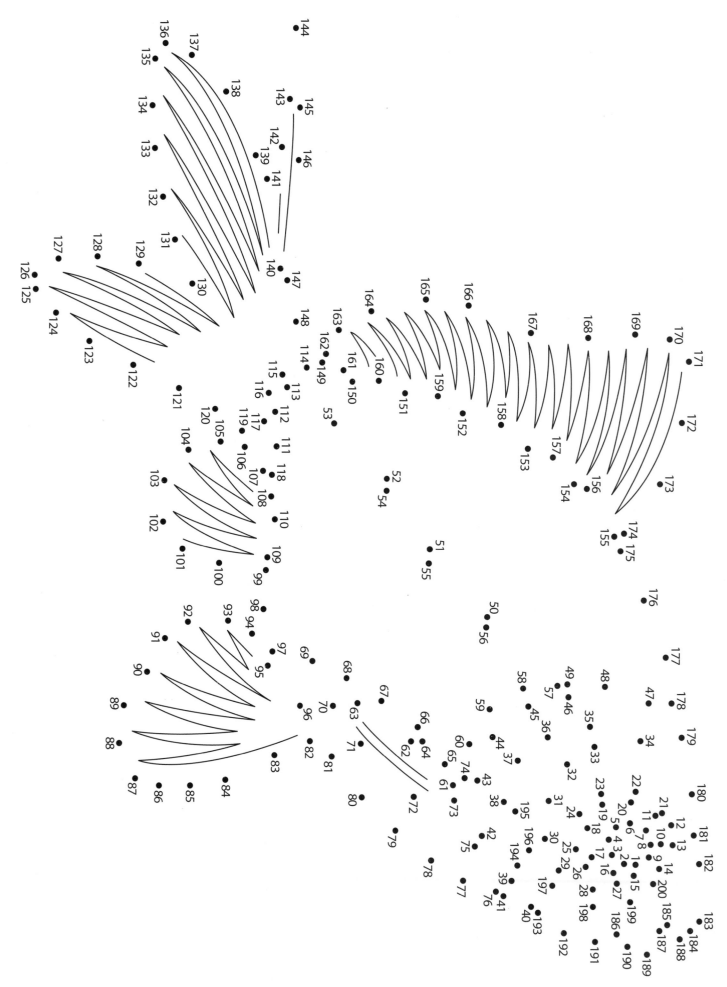

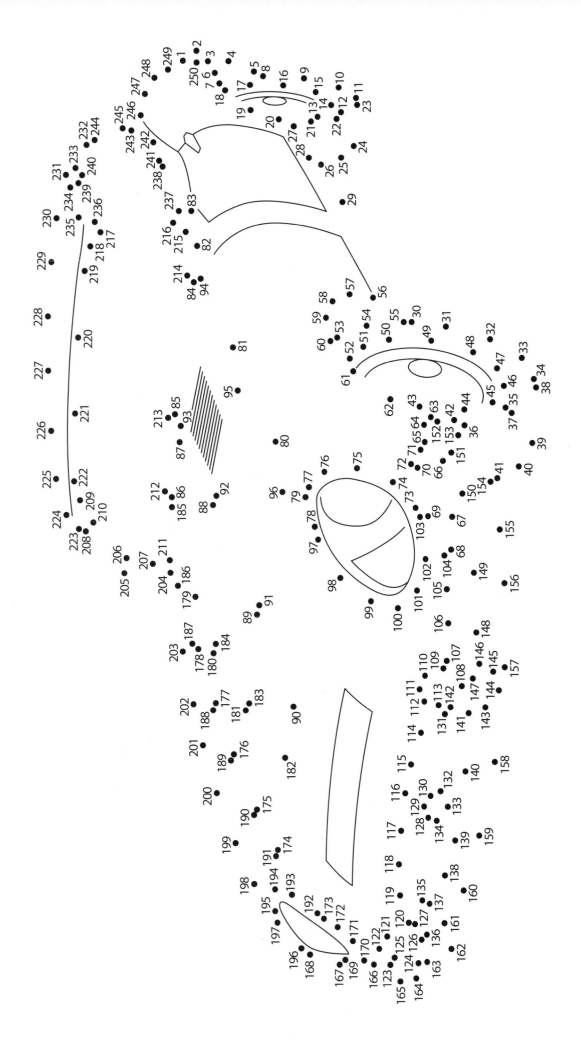

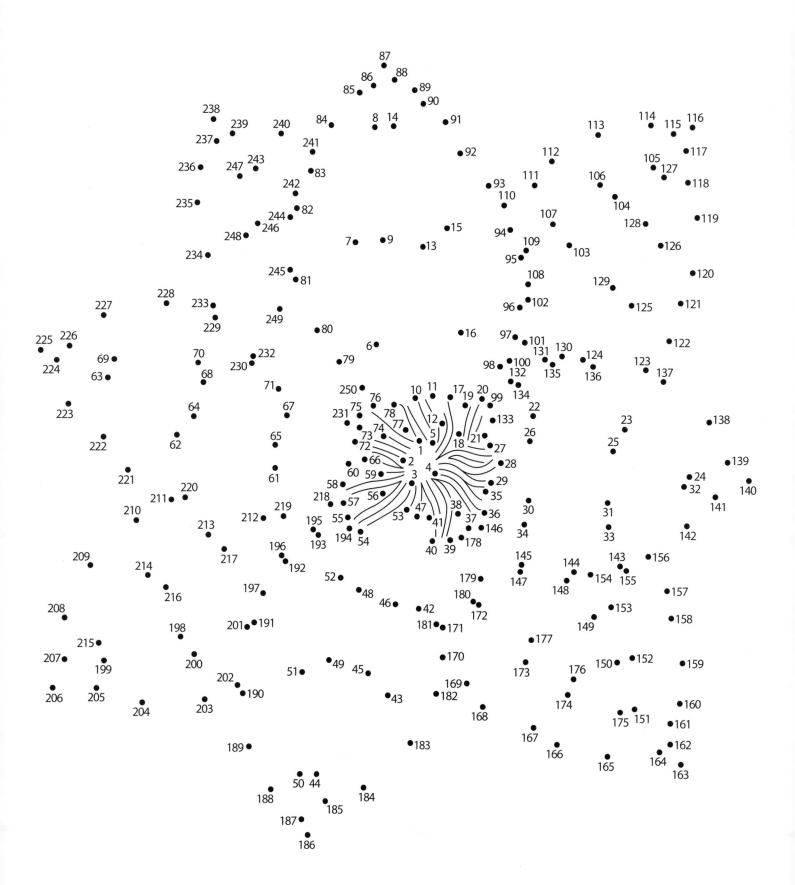

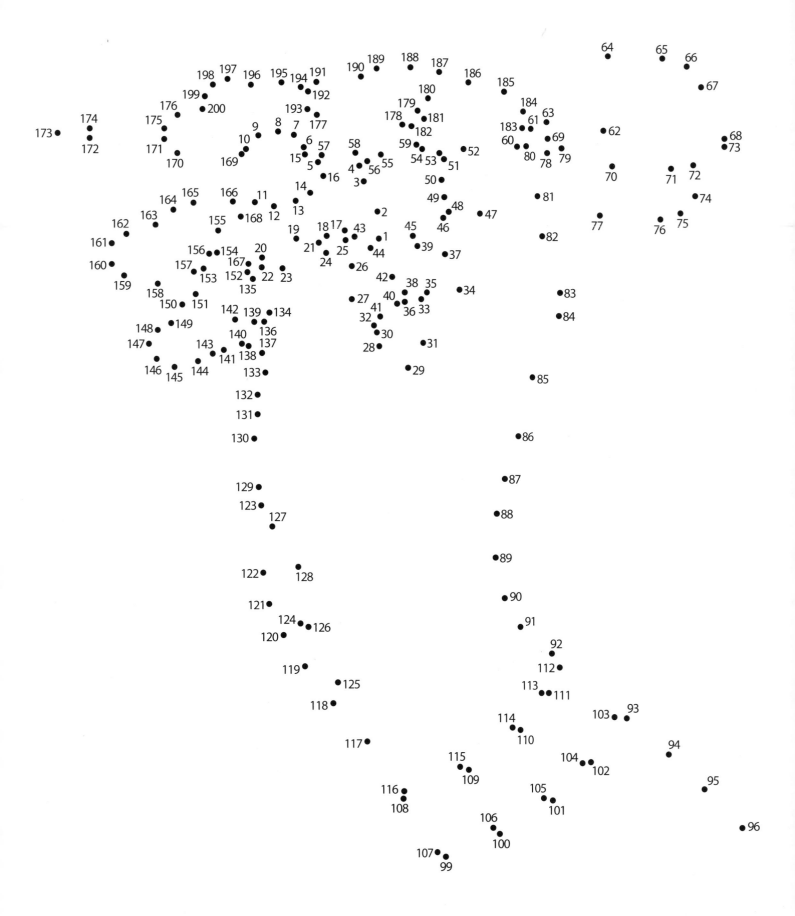

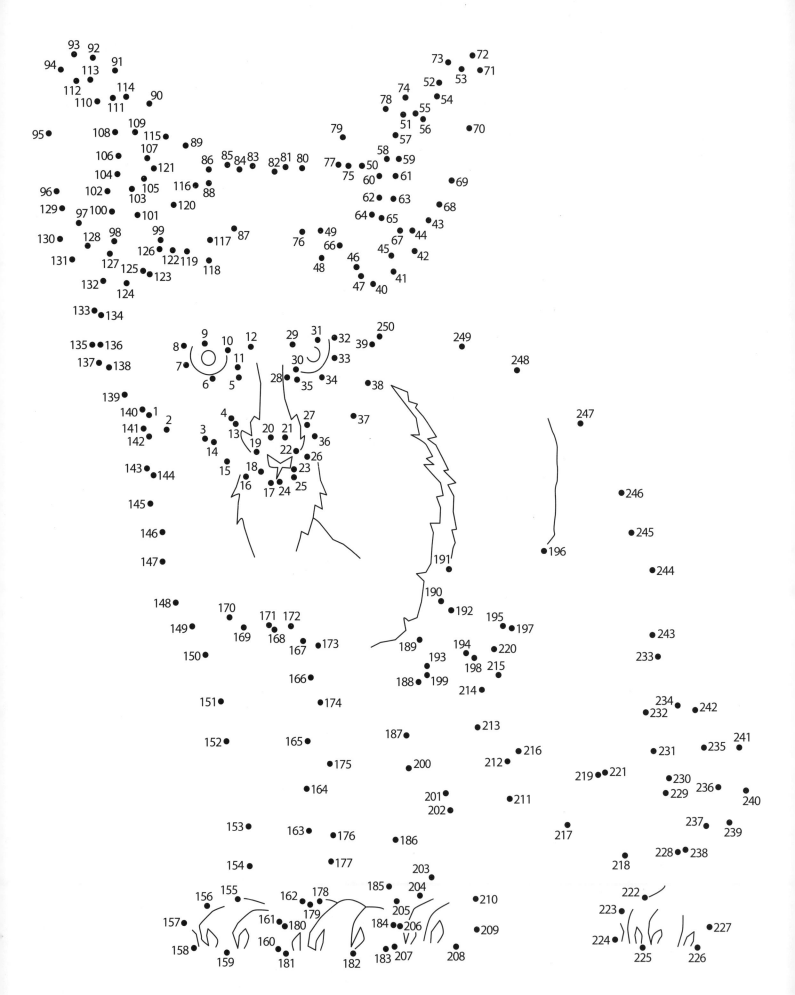

46

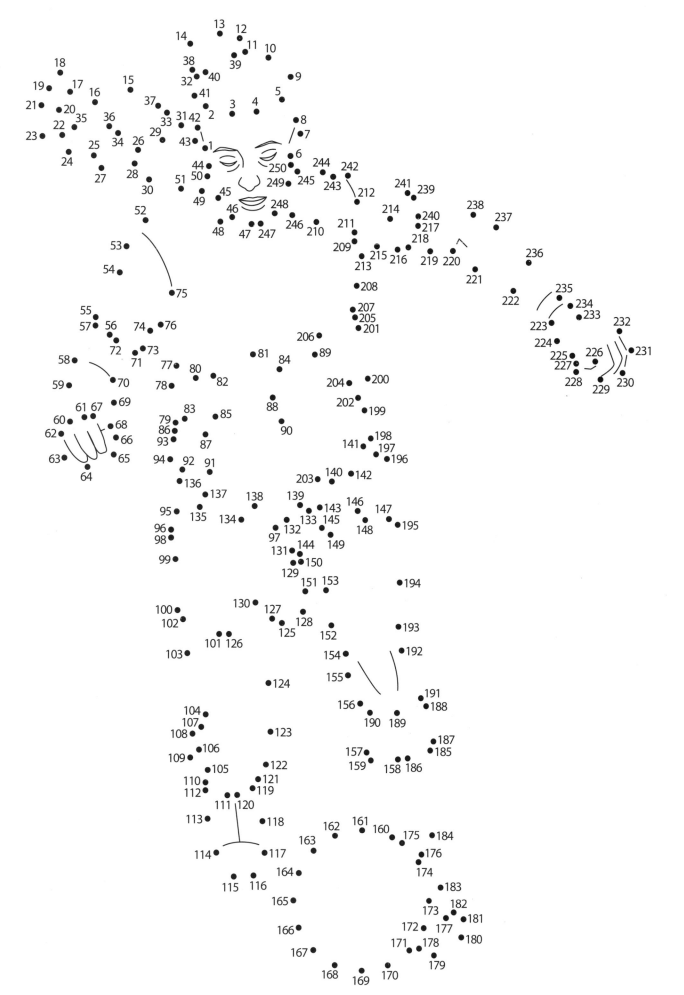

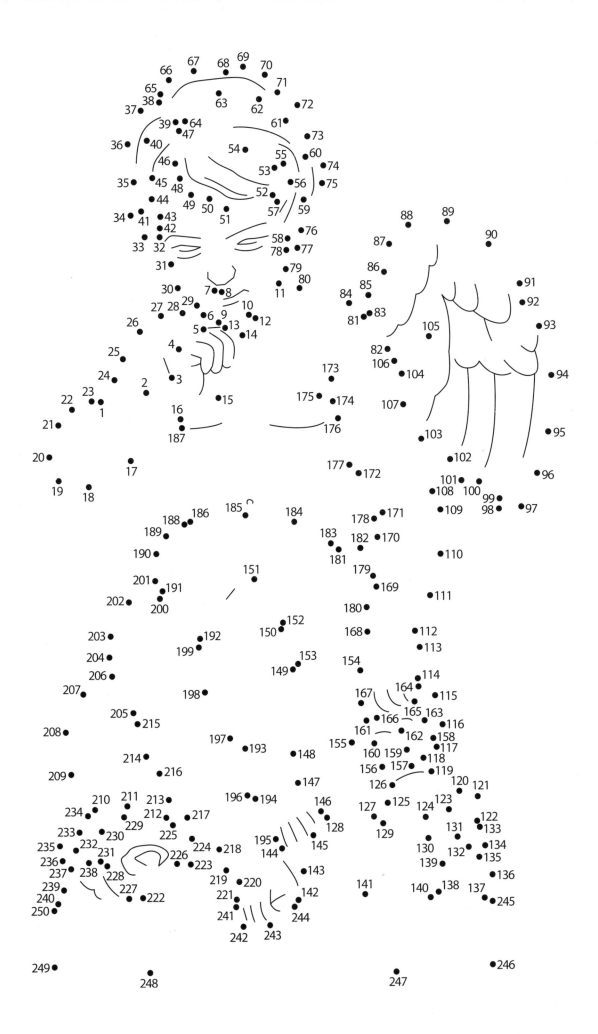

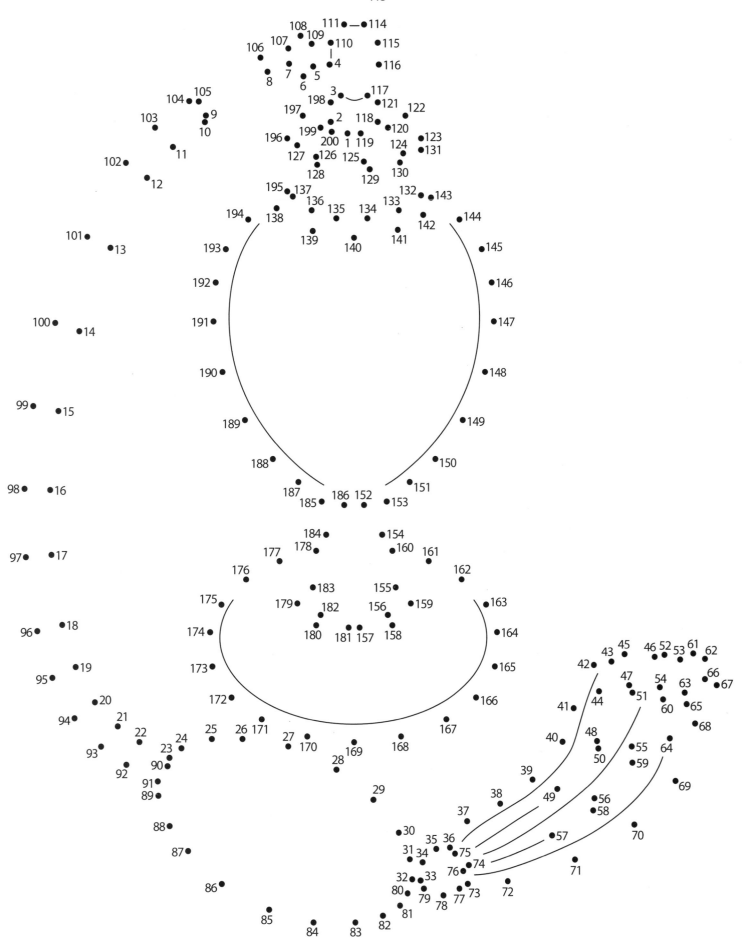

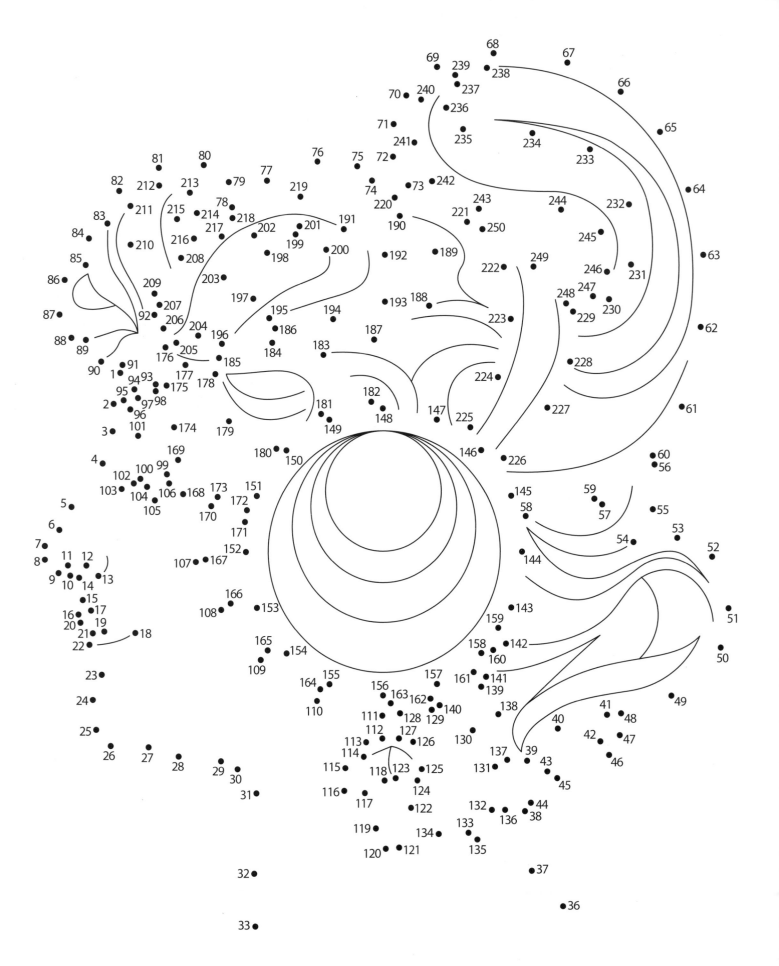

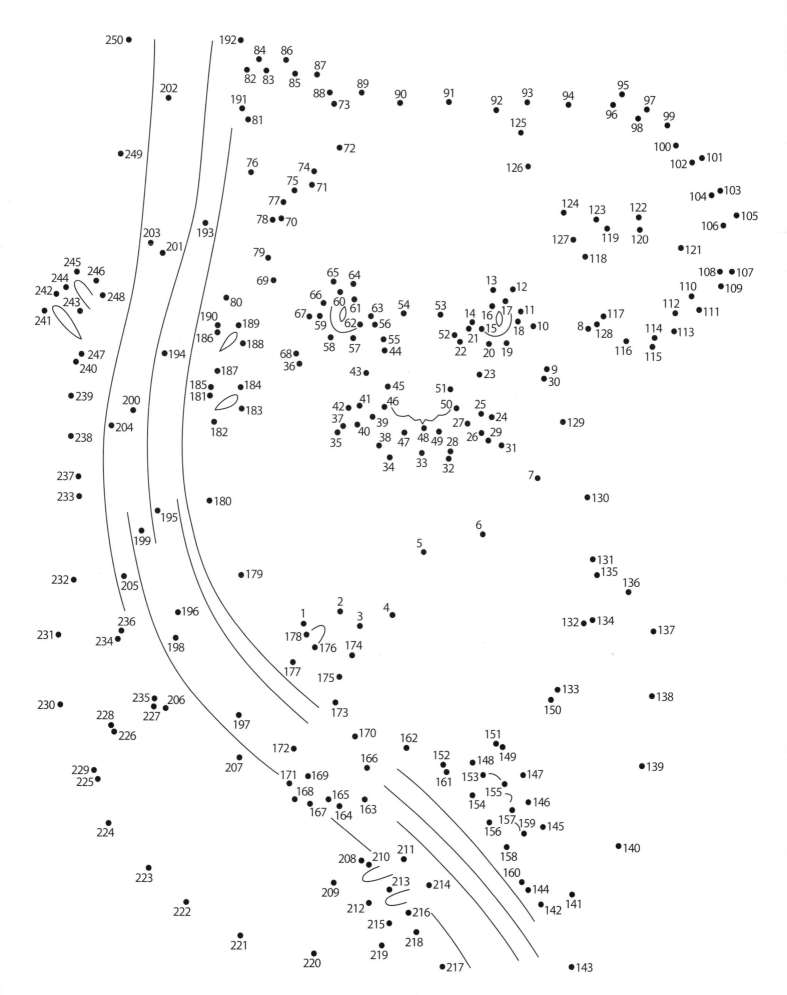

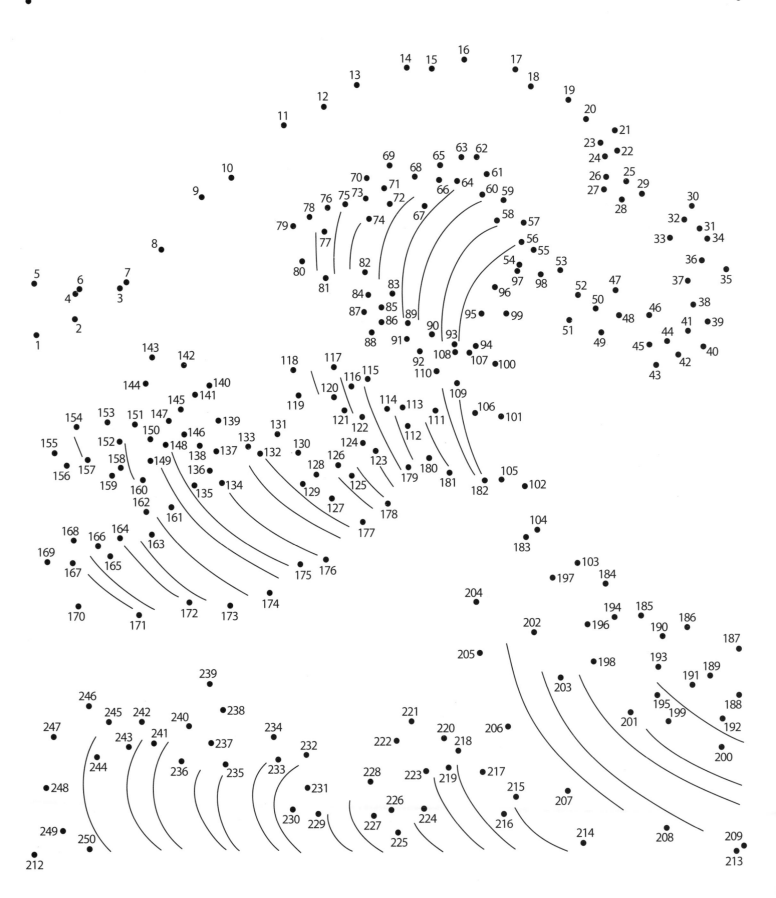

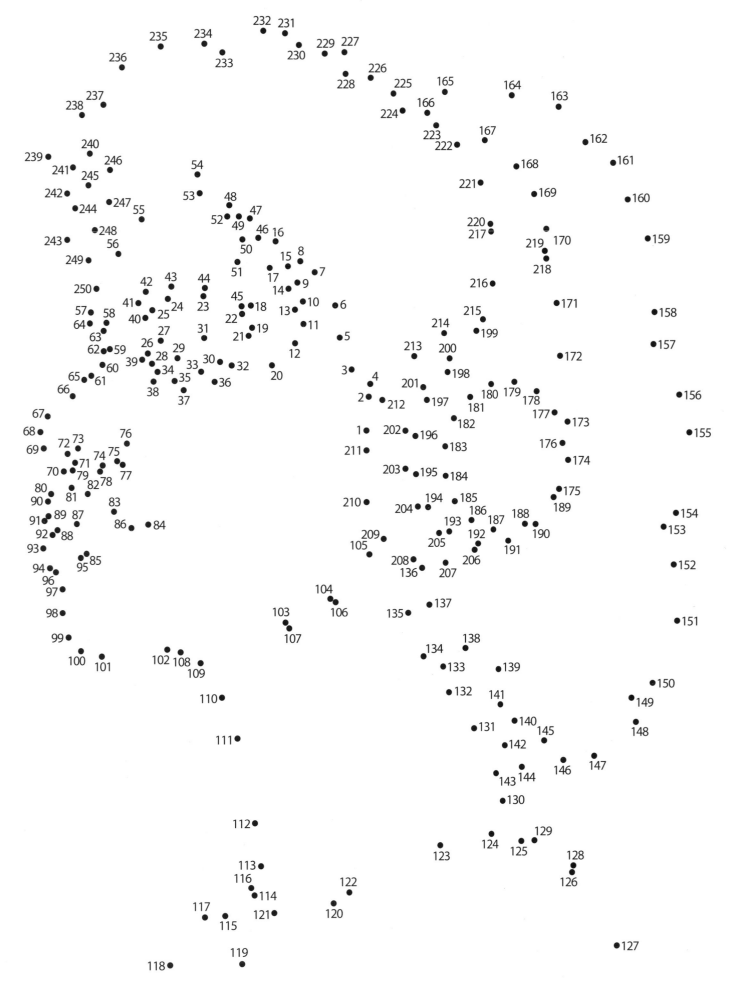

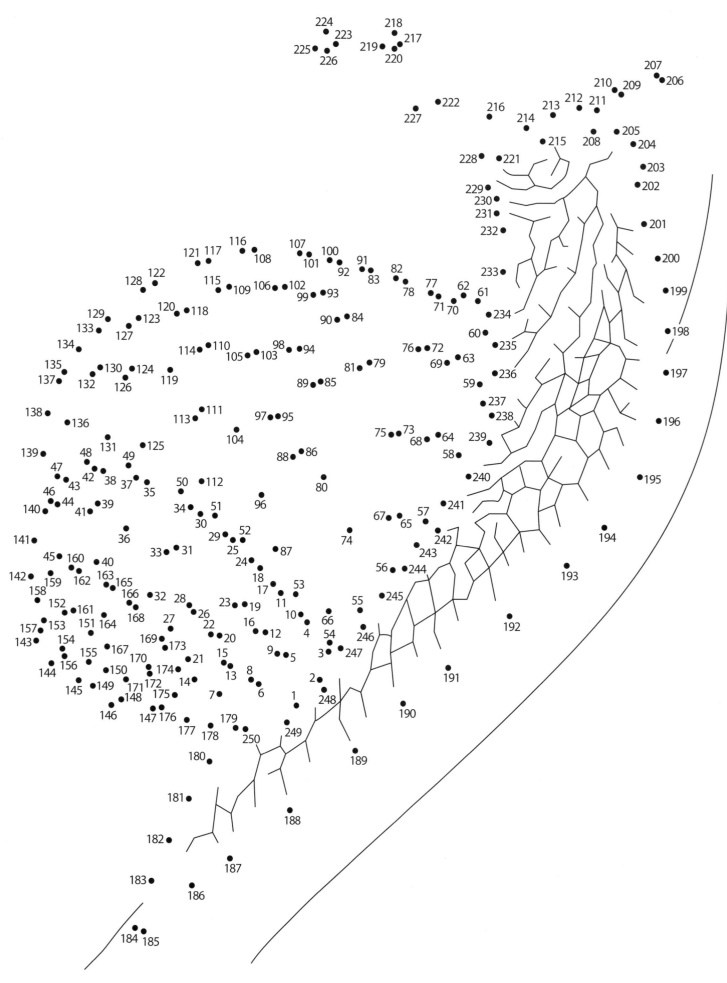

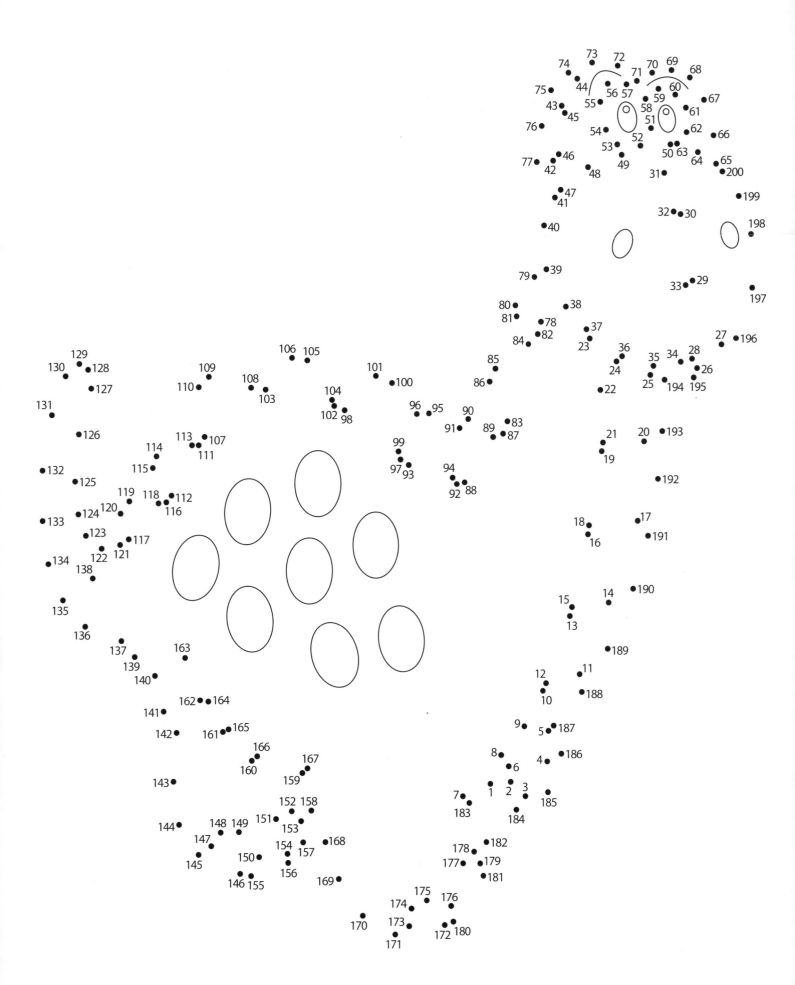

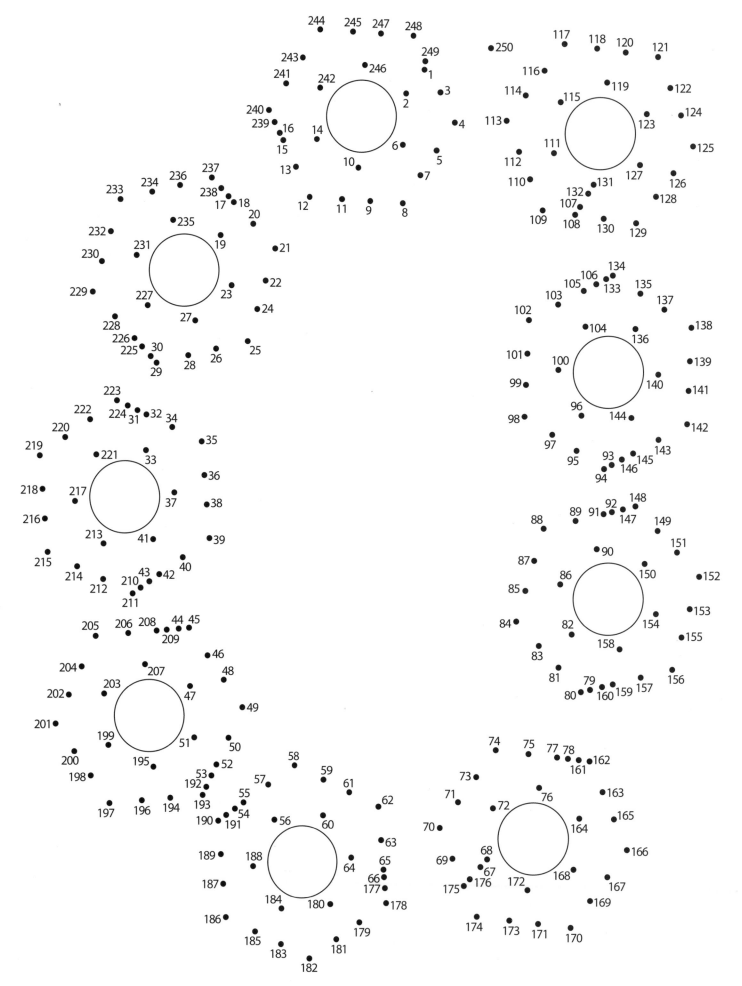

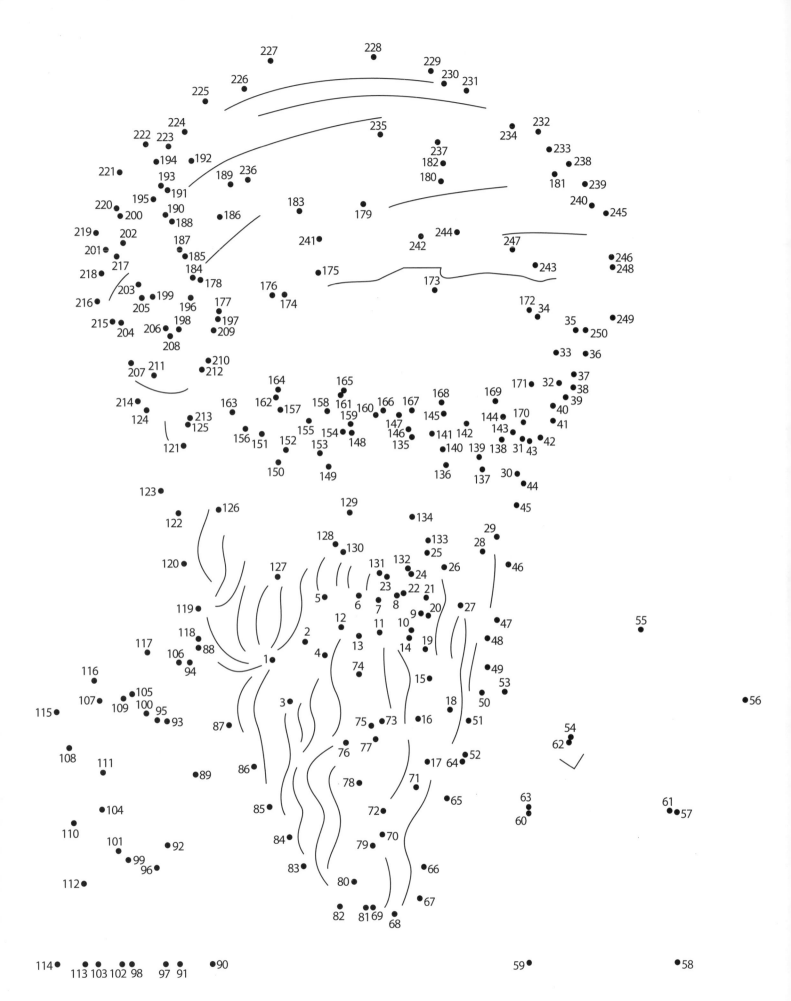

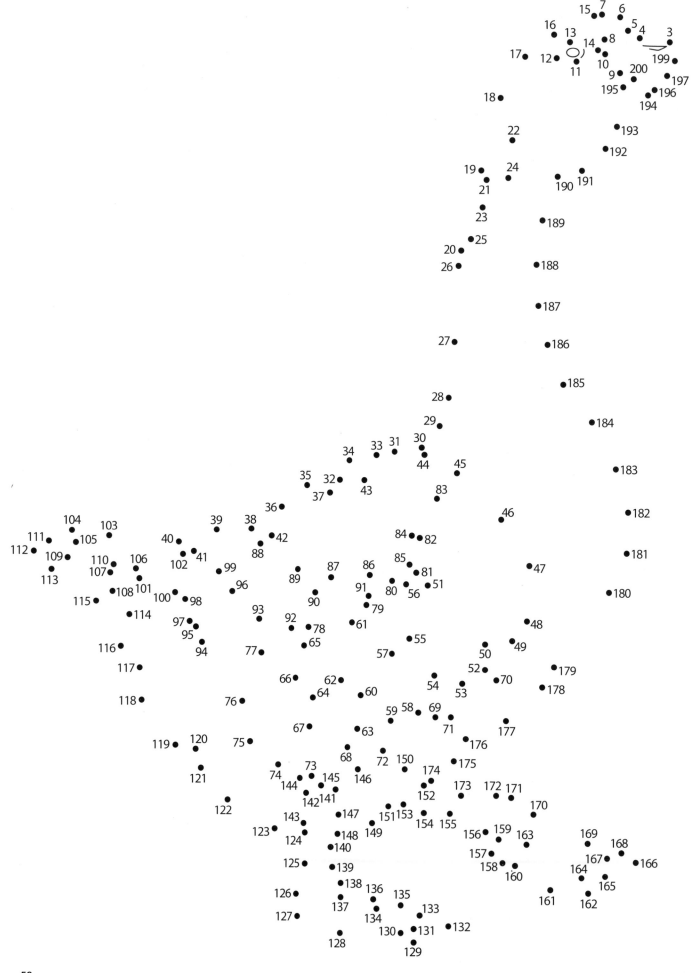

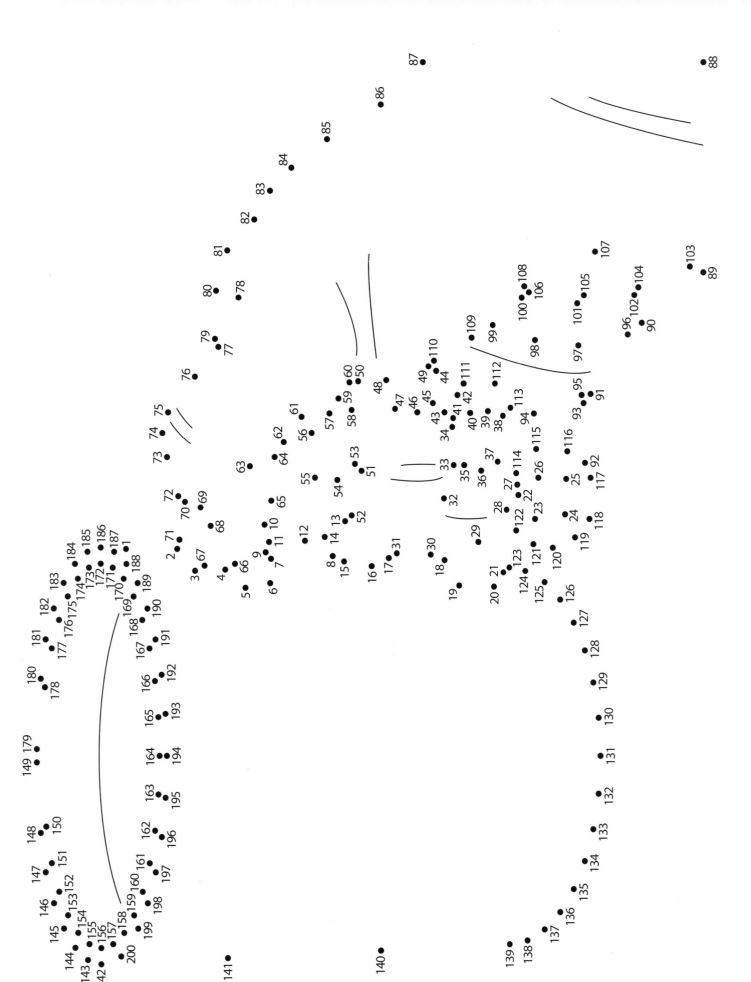

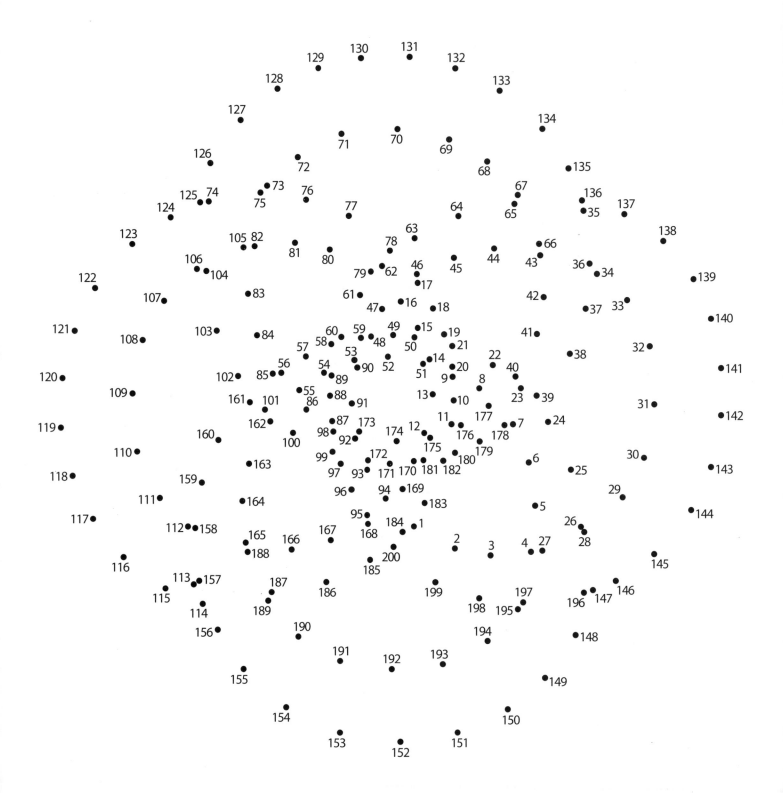

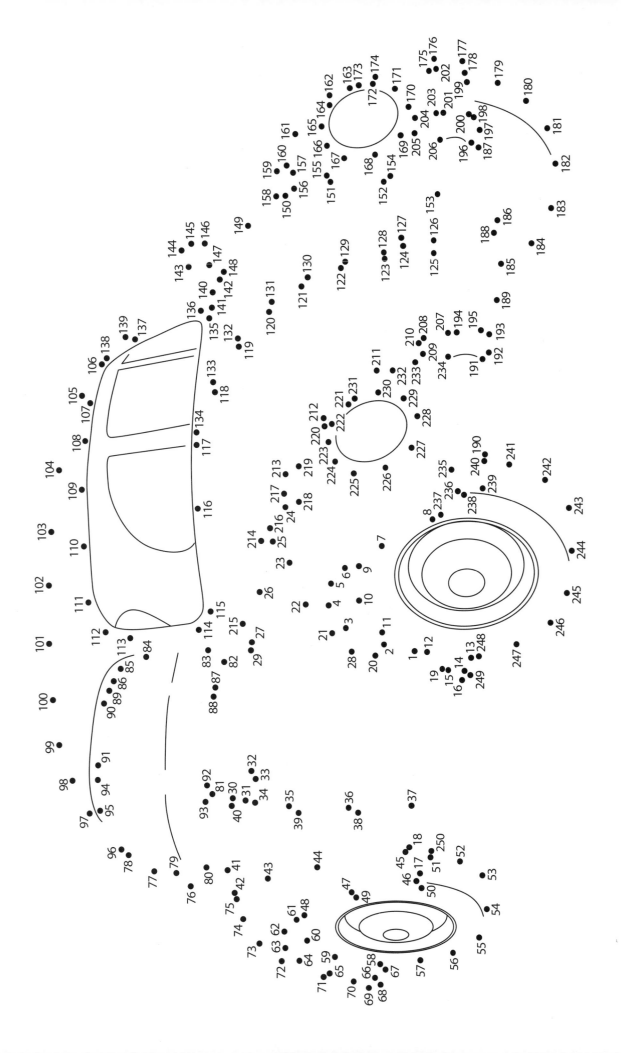

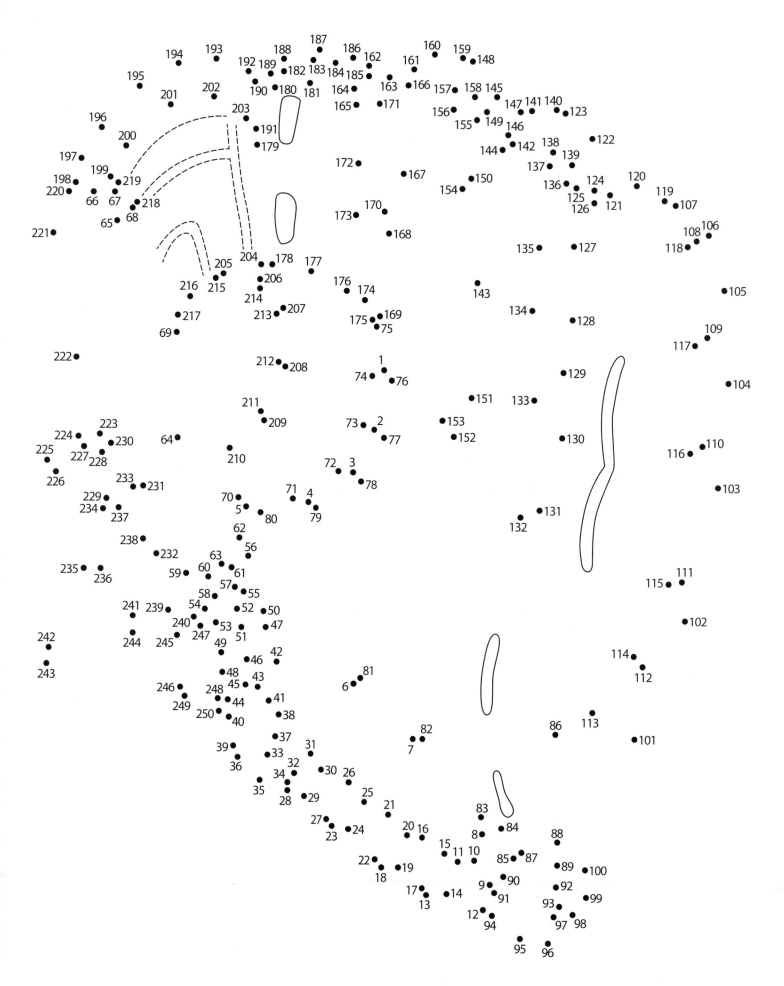

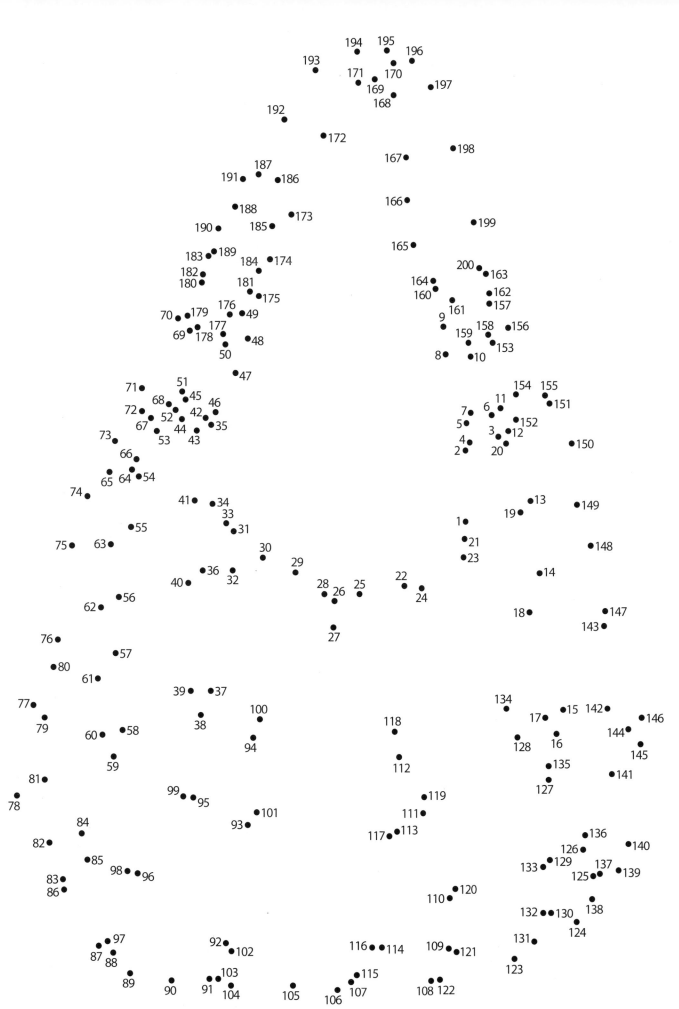

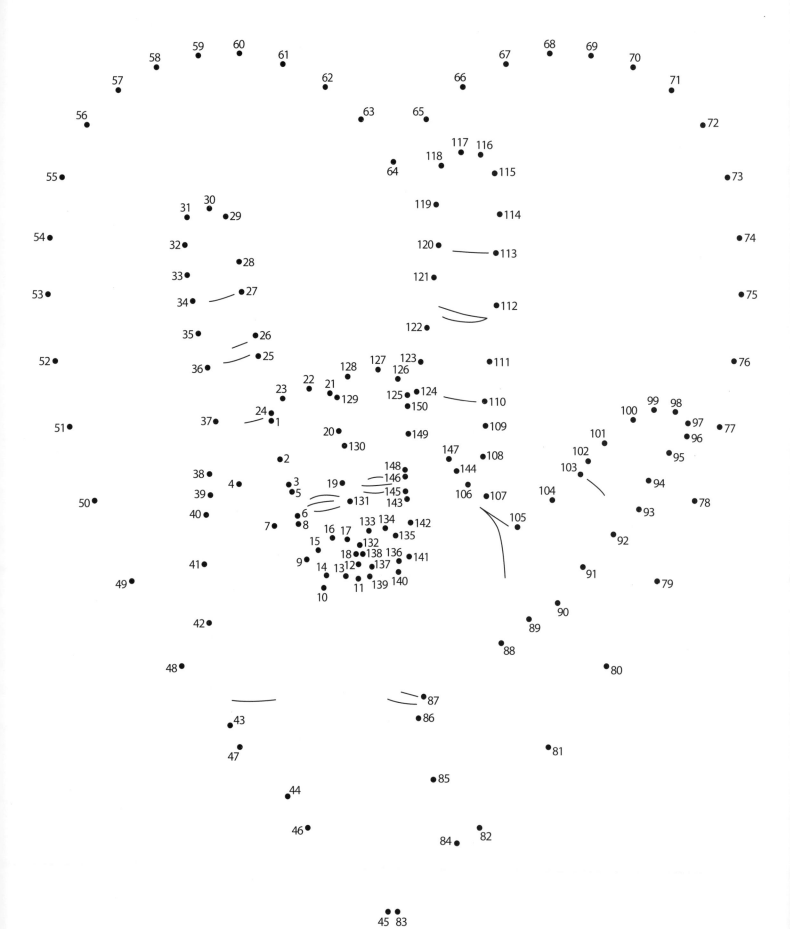

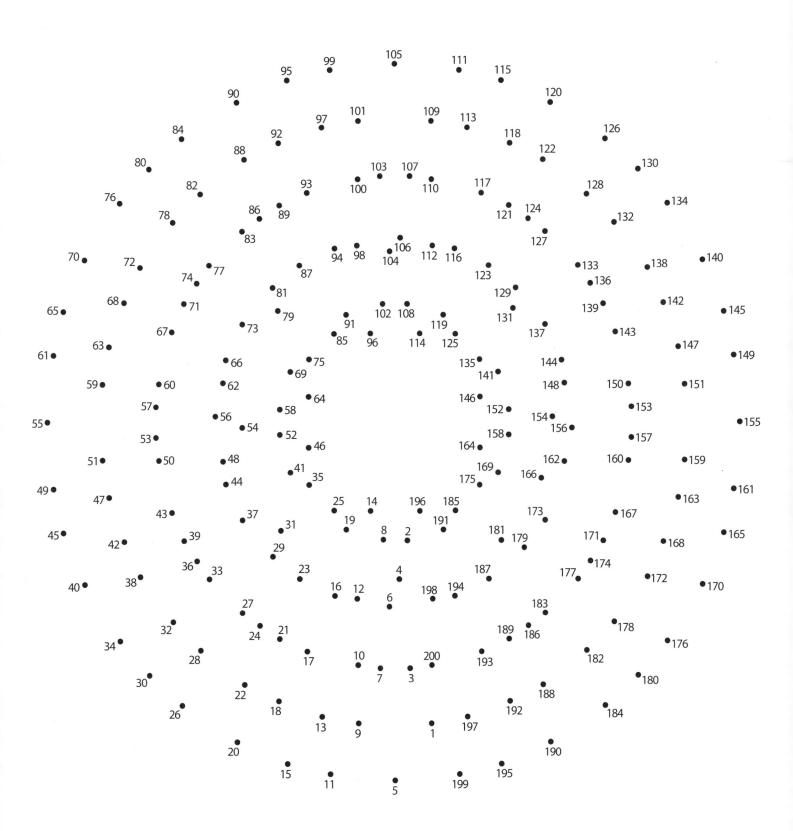

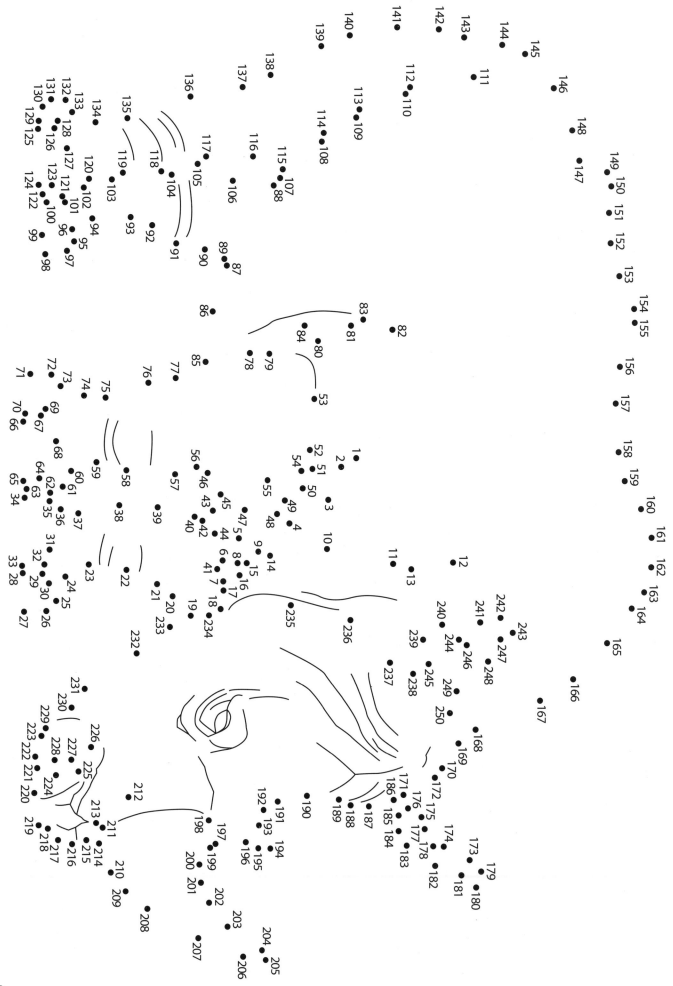

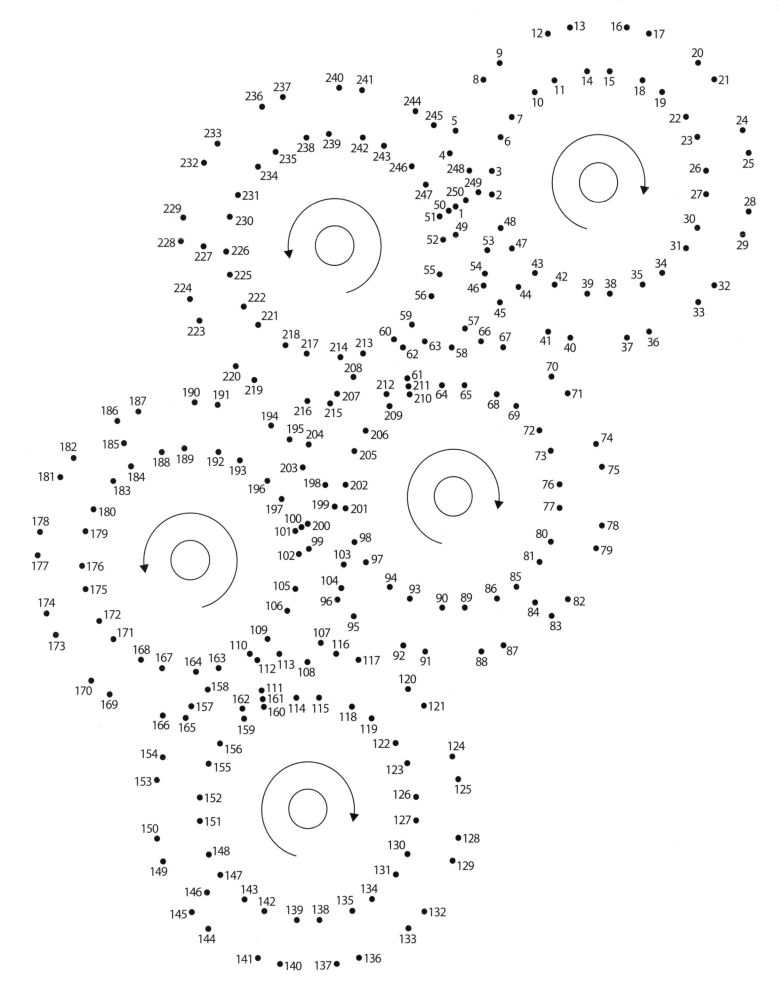

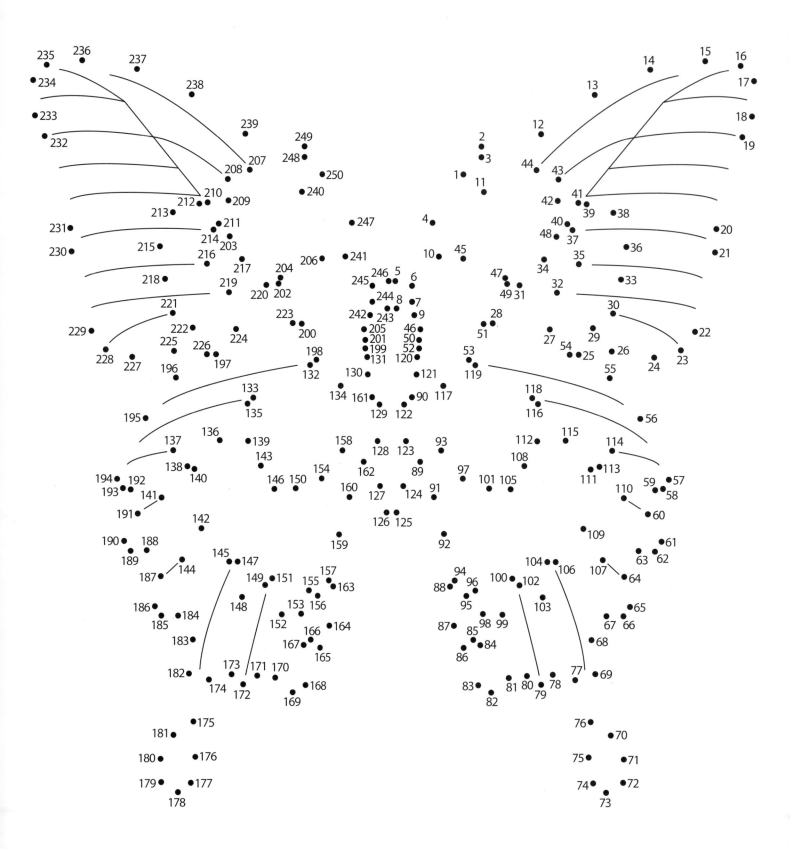

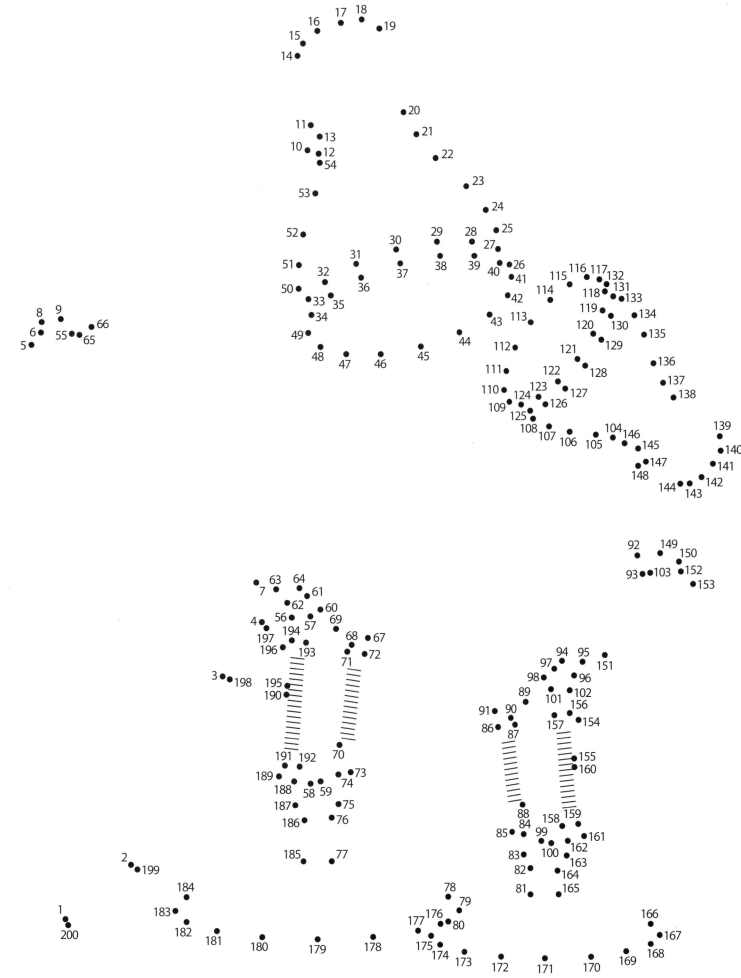

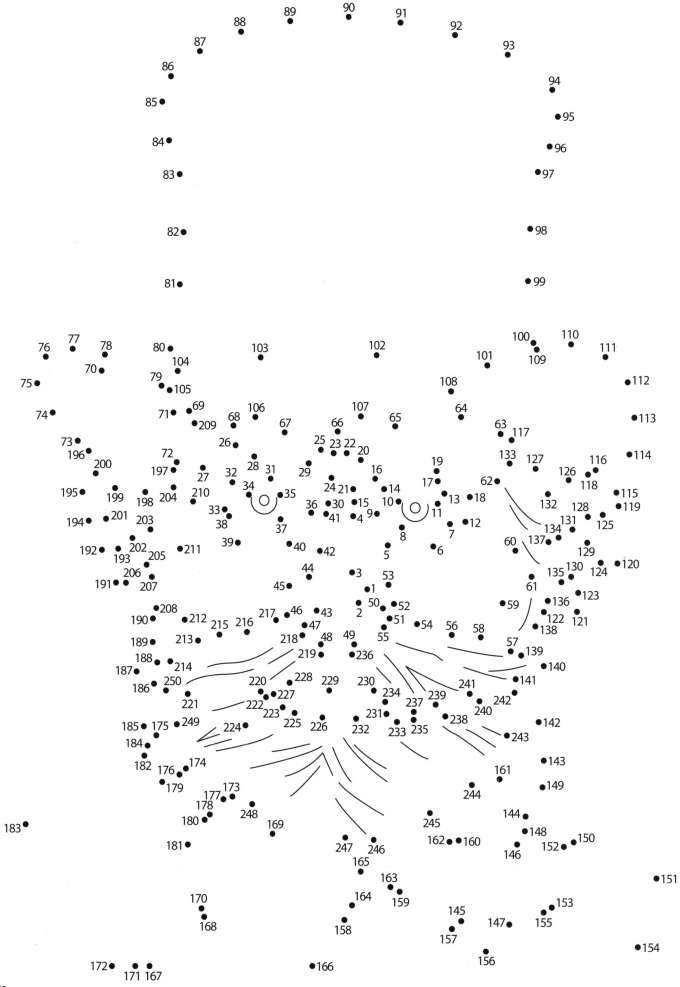

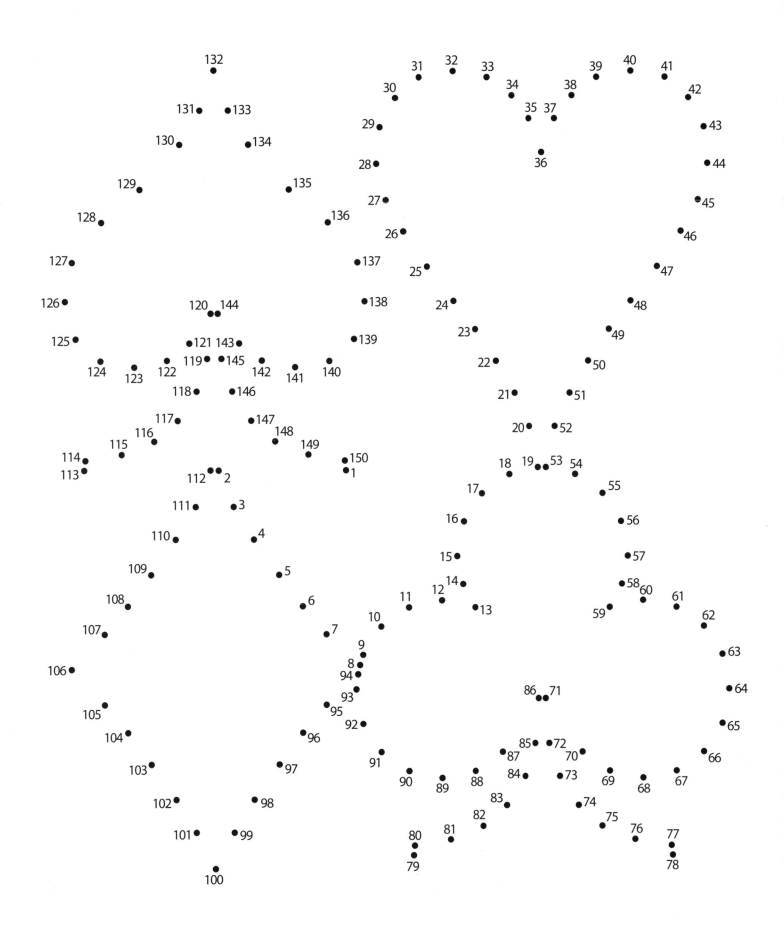

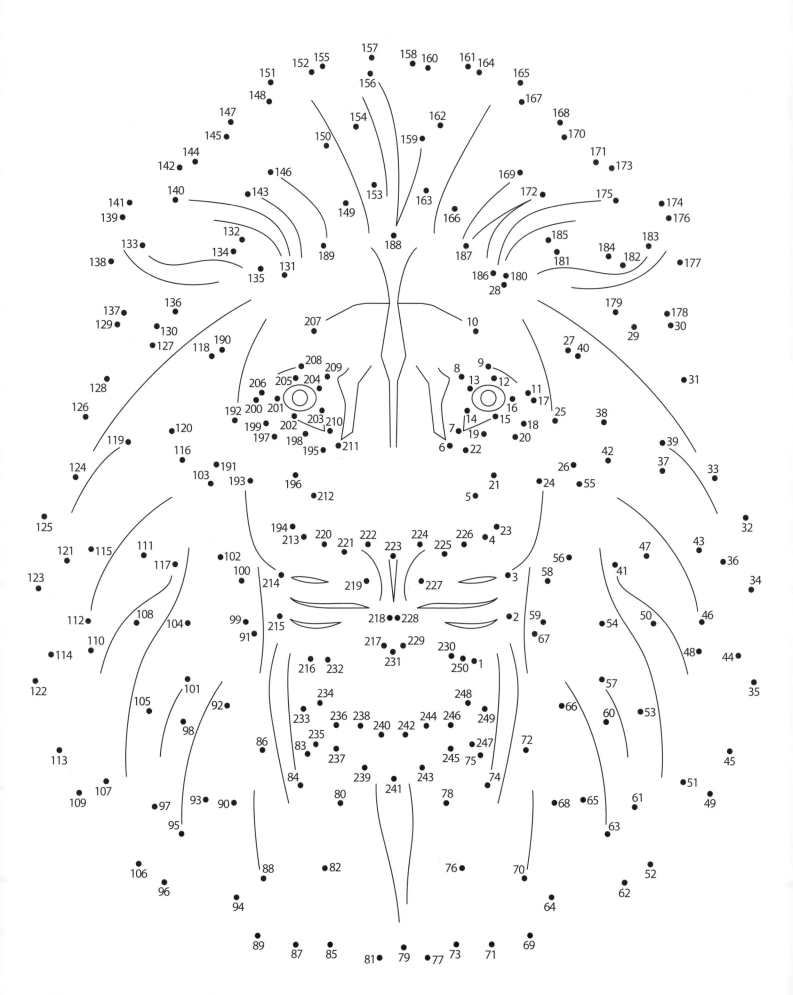

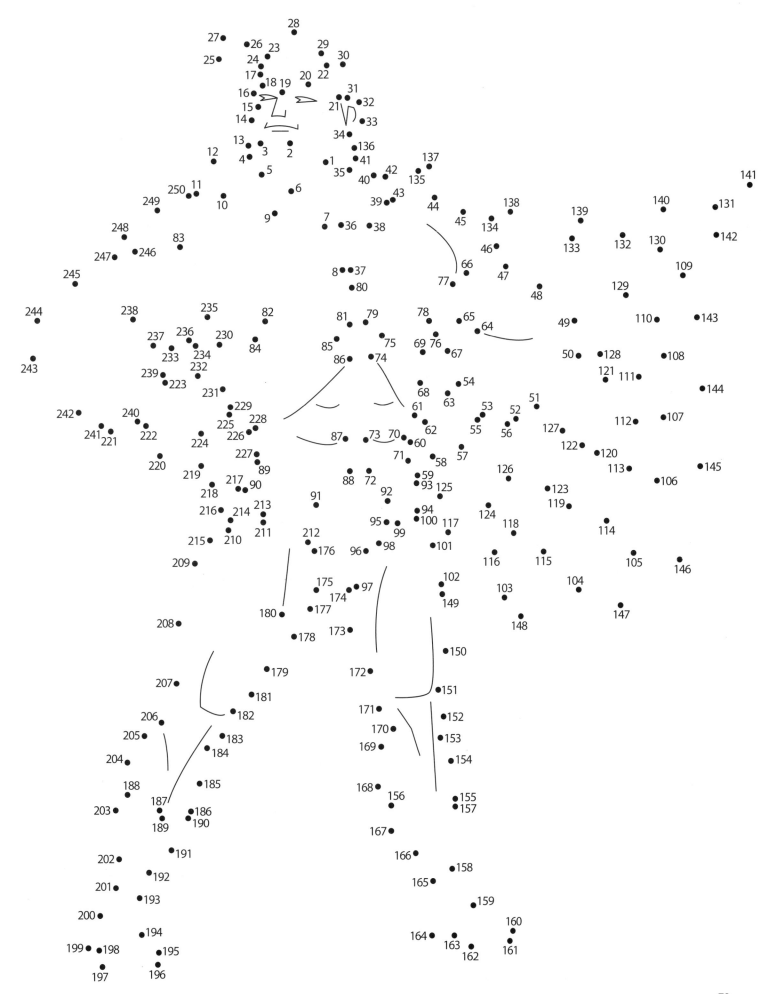

73

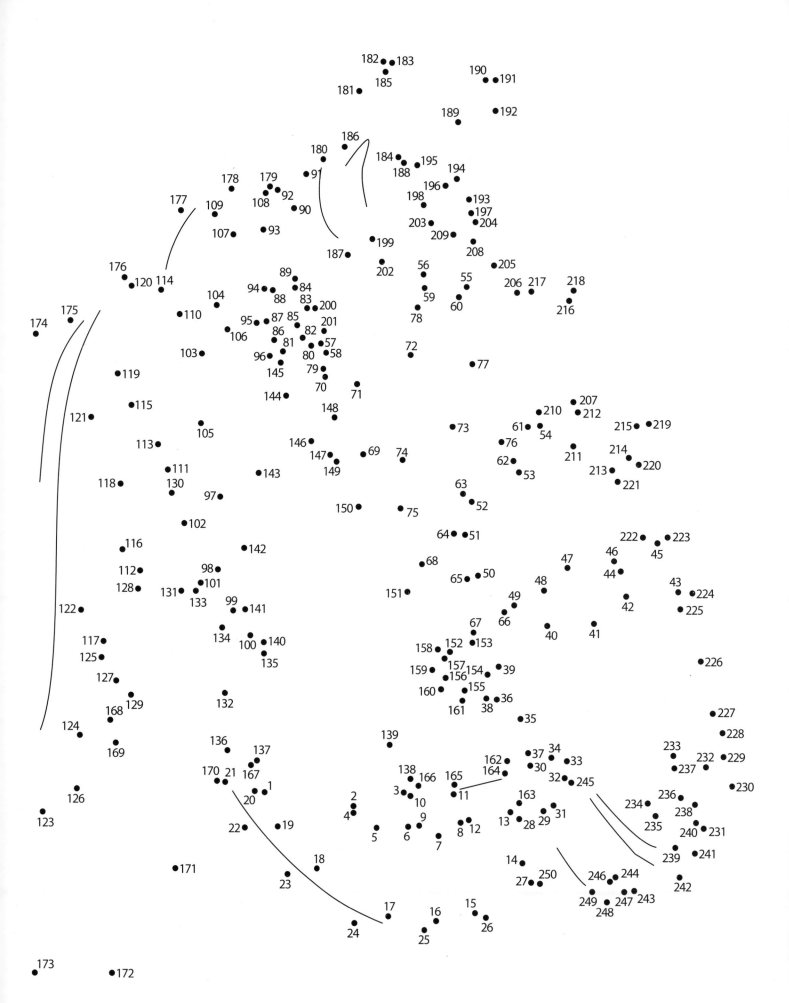

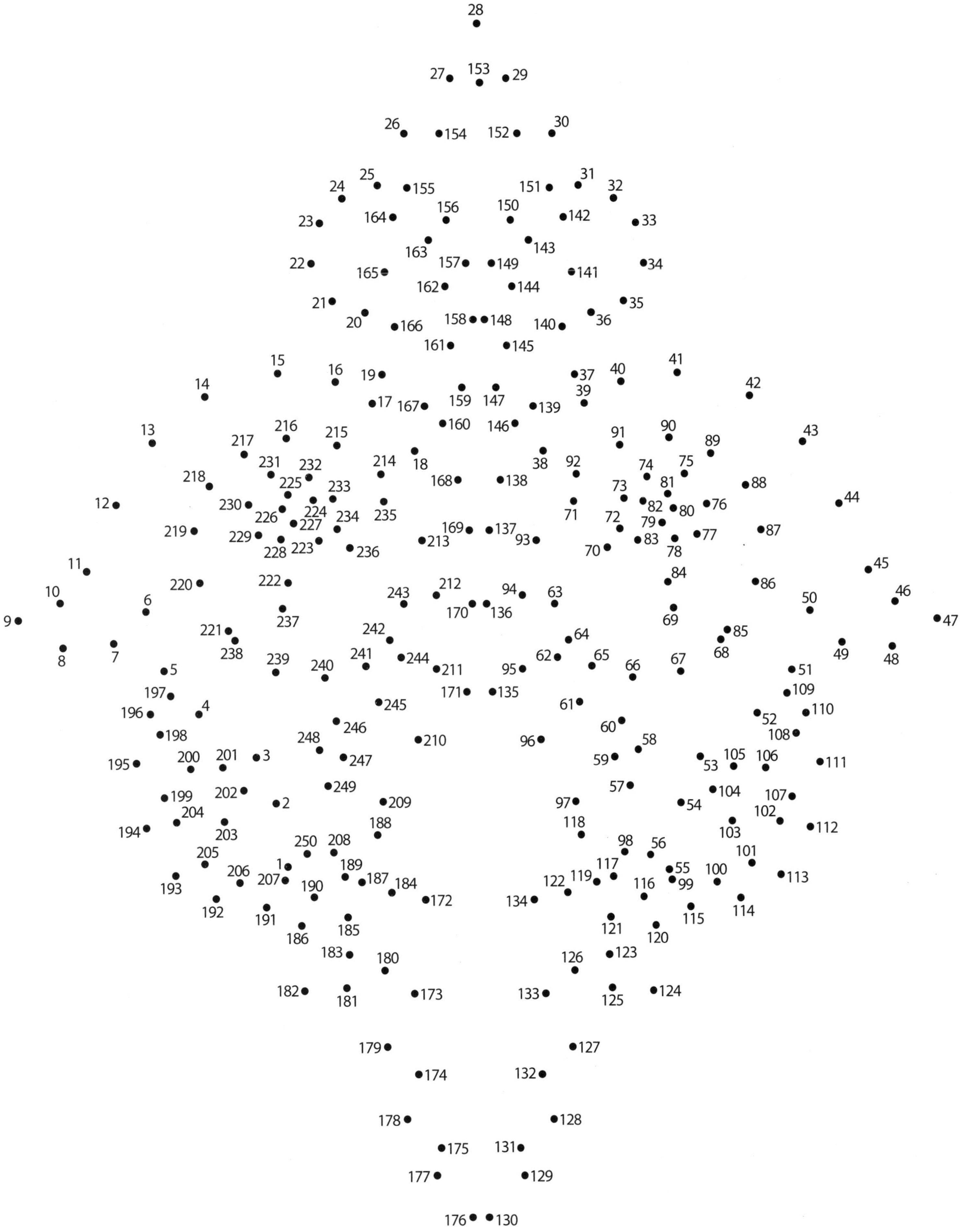

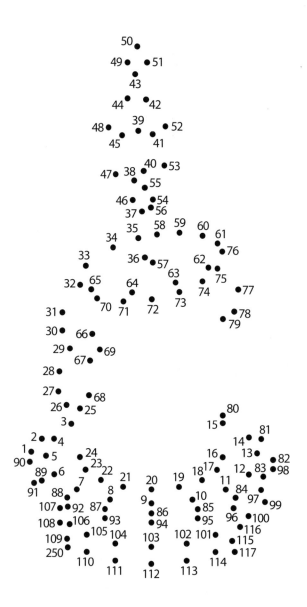
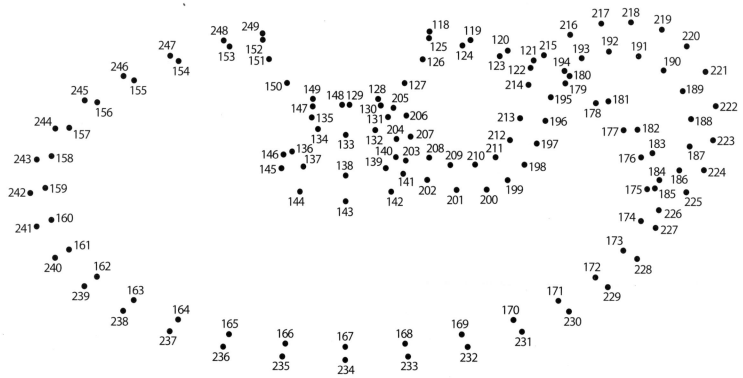

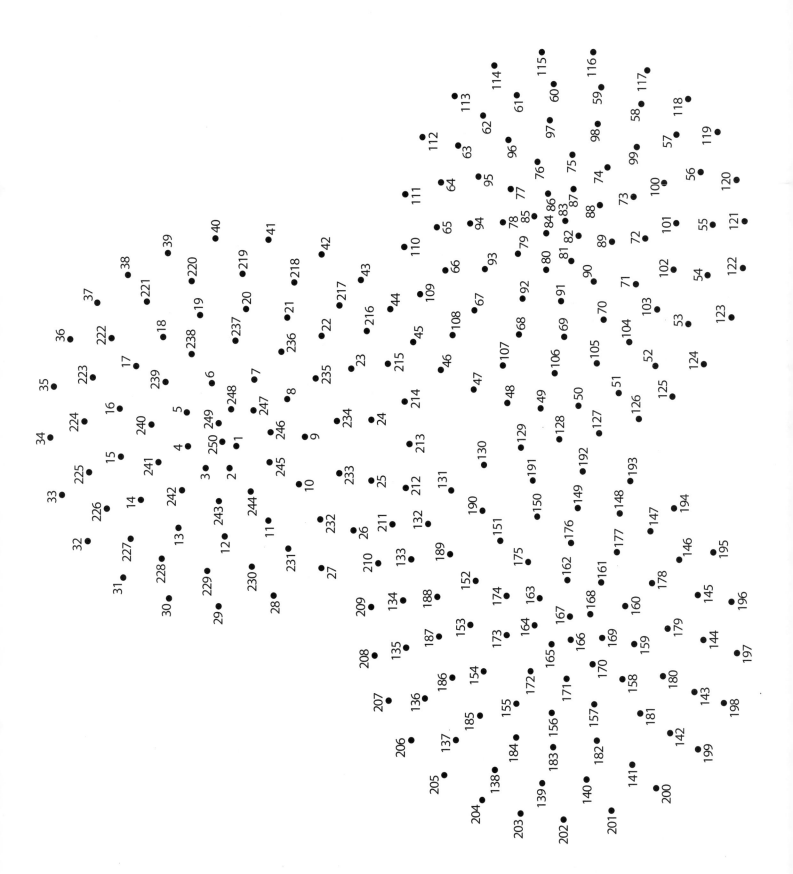

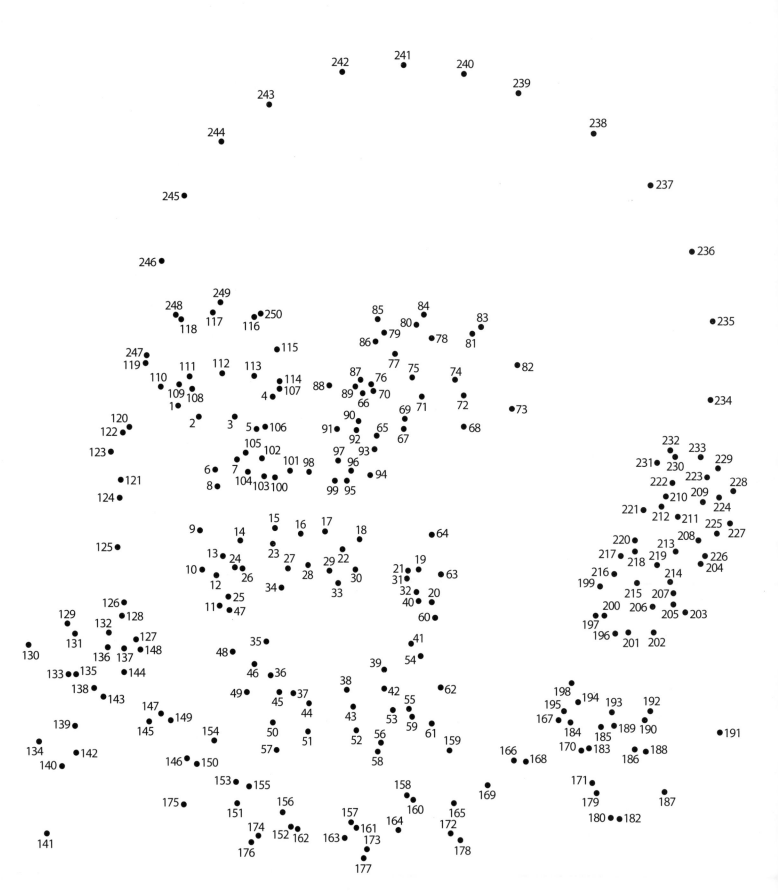

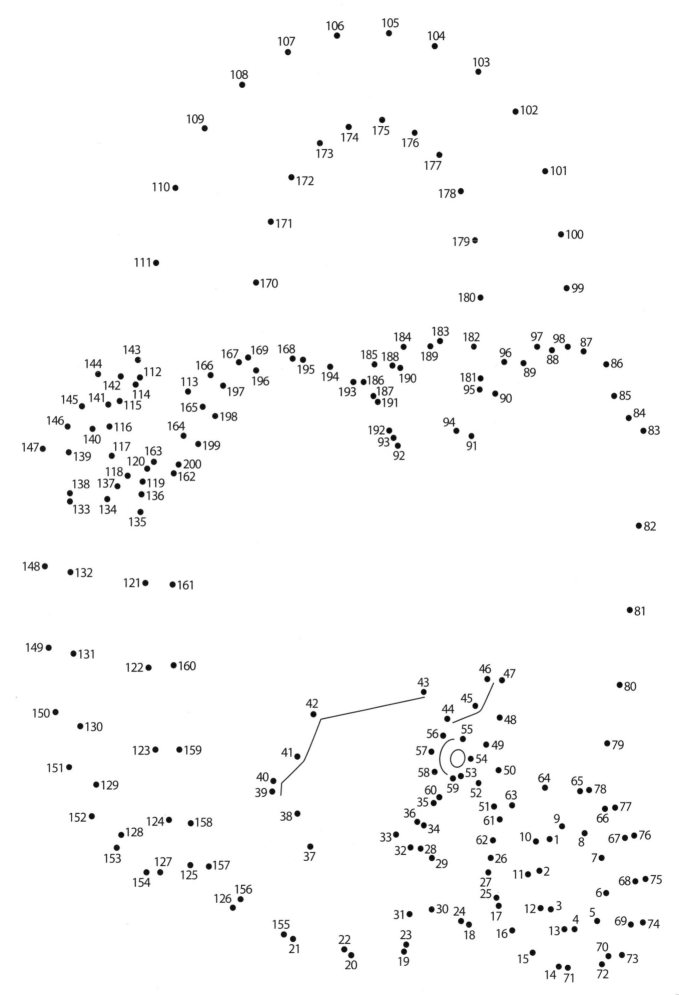

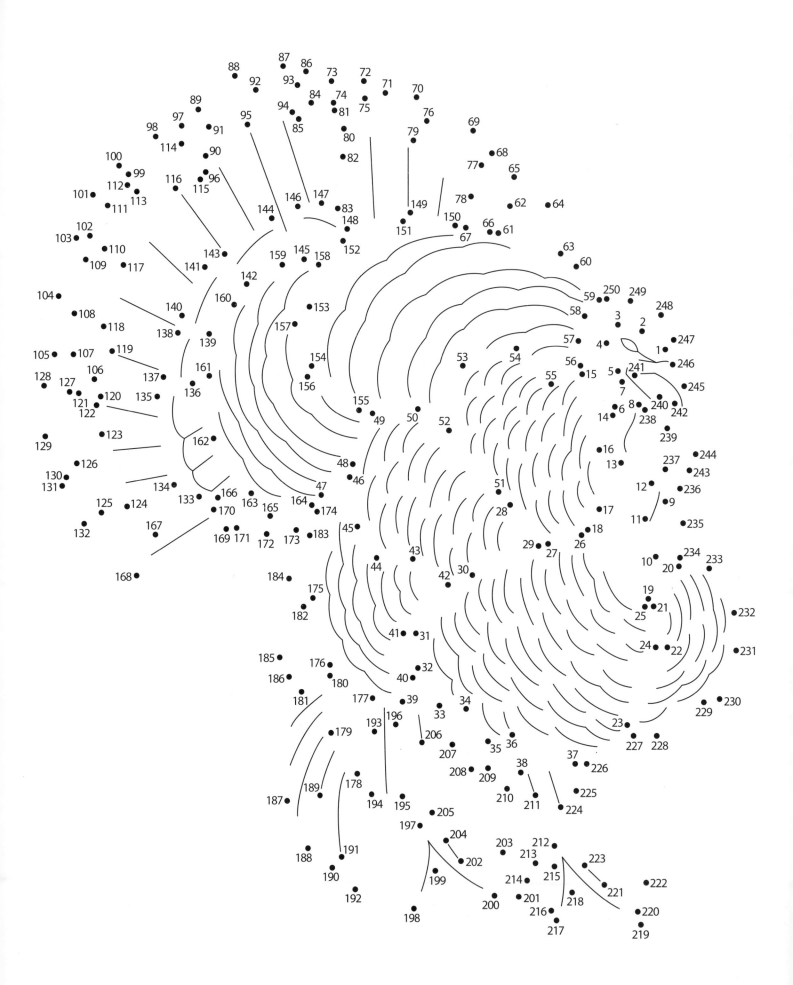

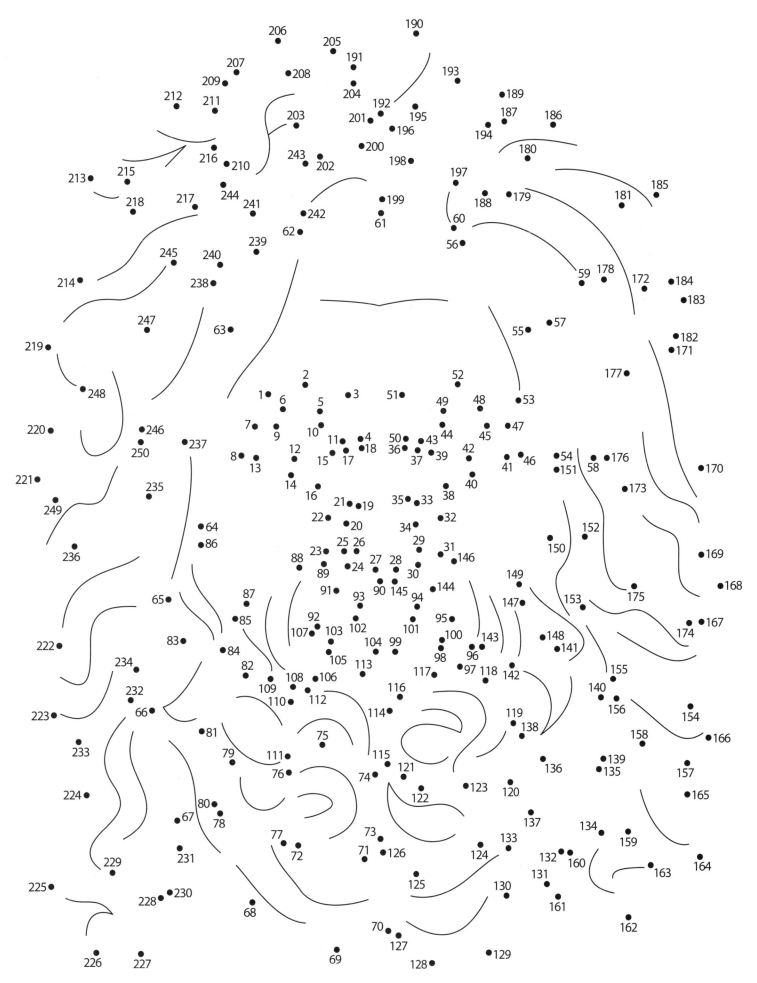

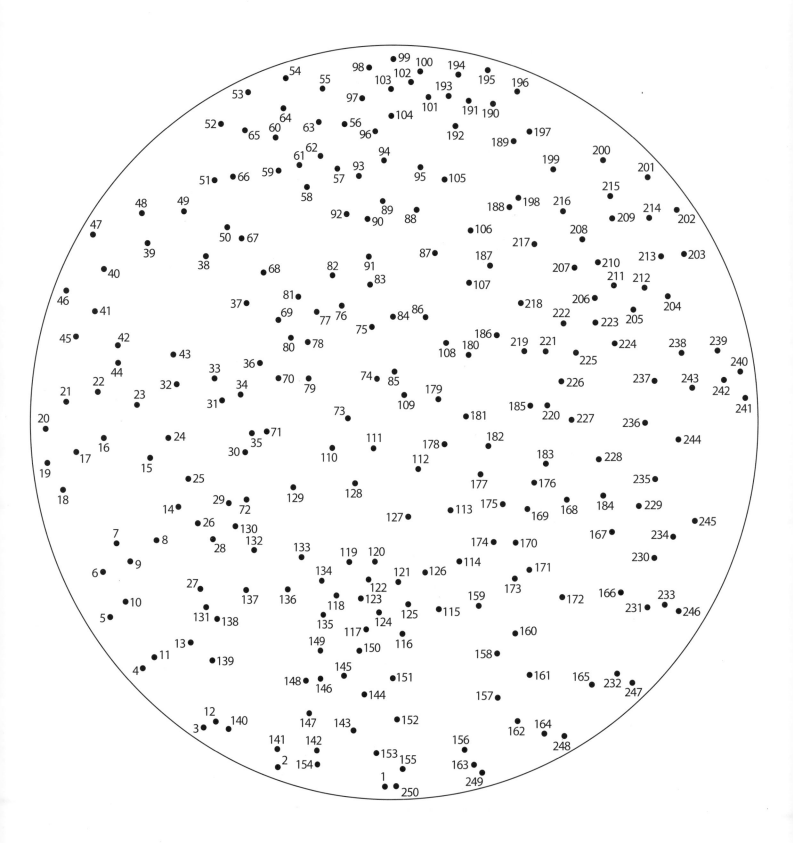

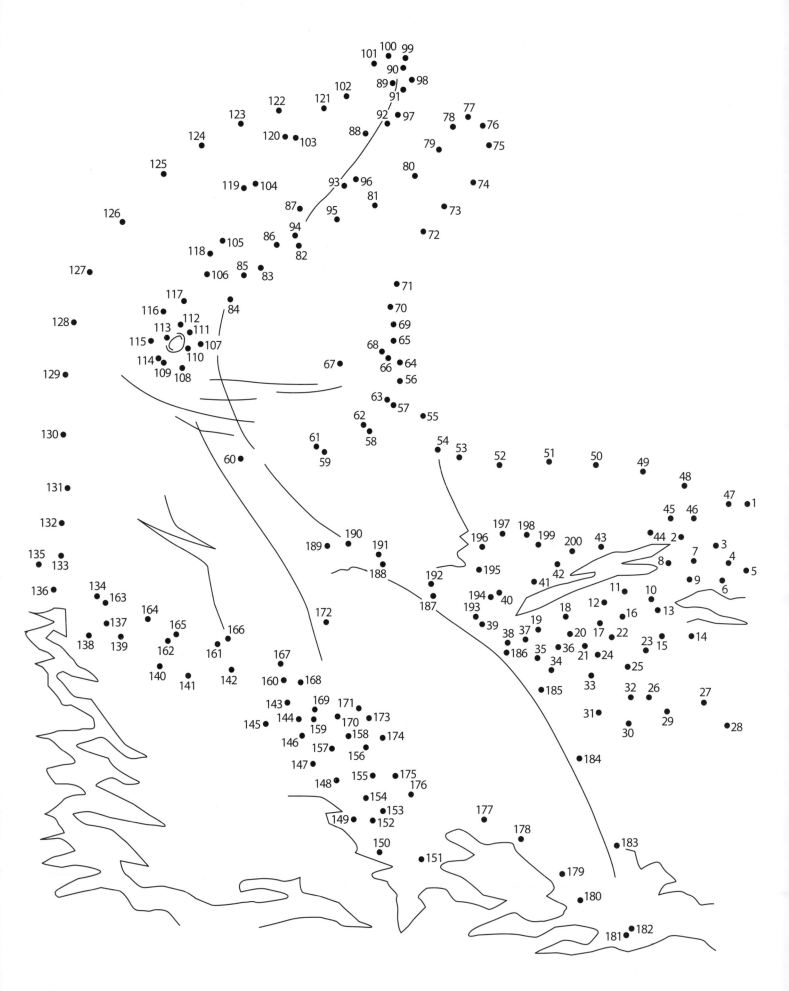

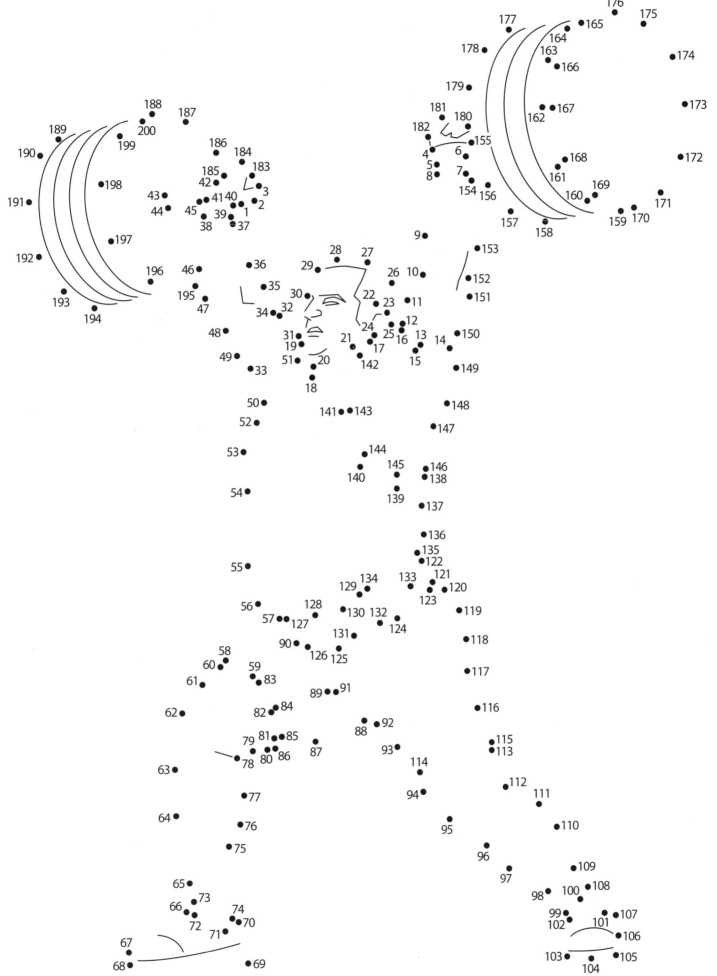

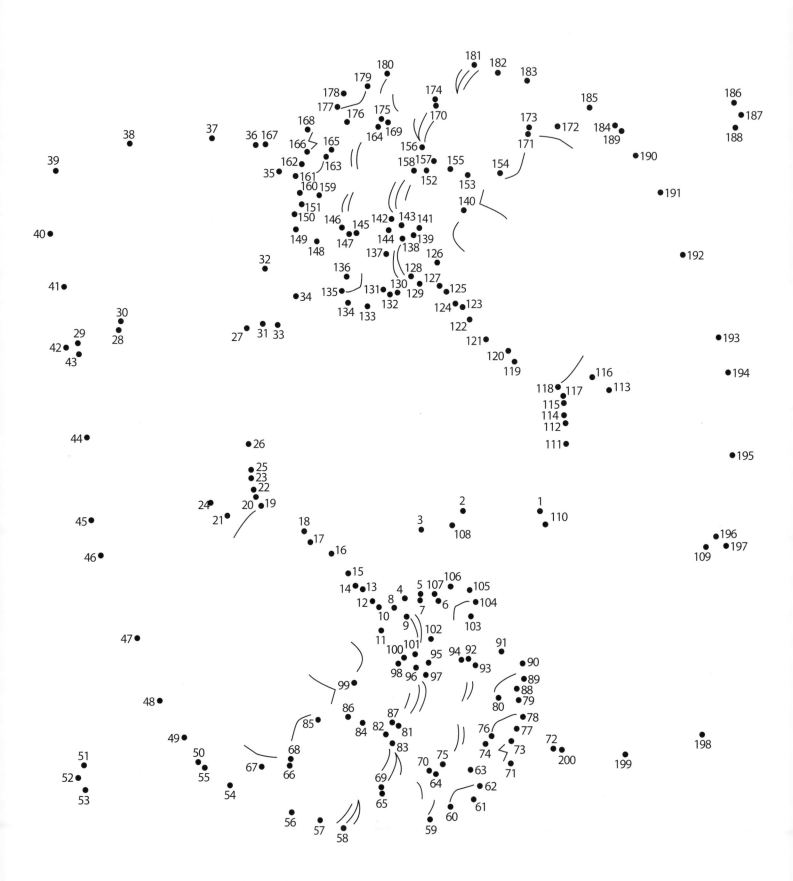

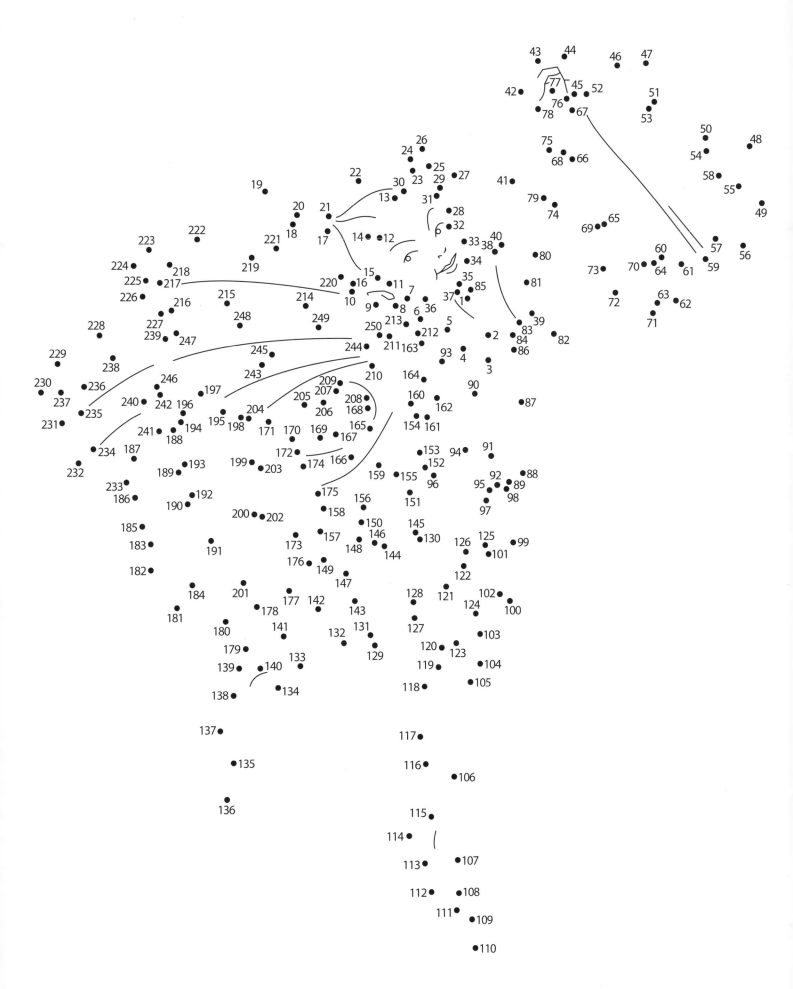

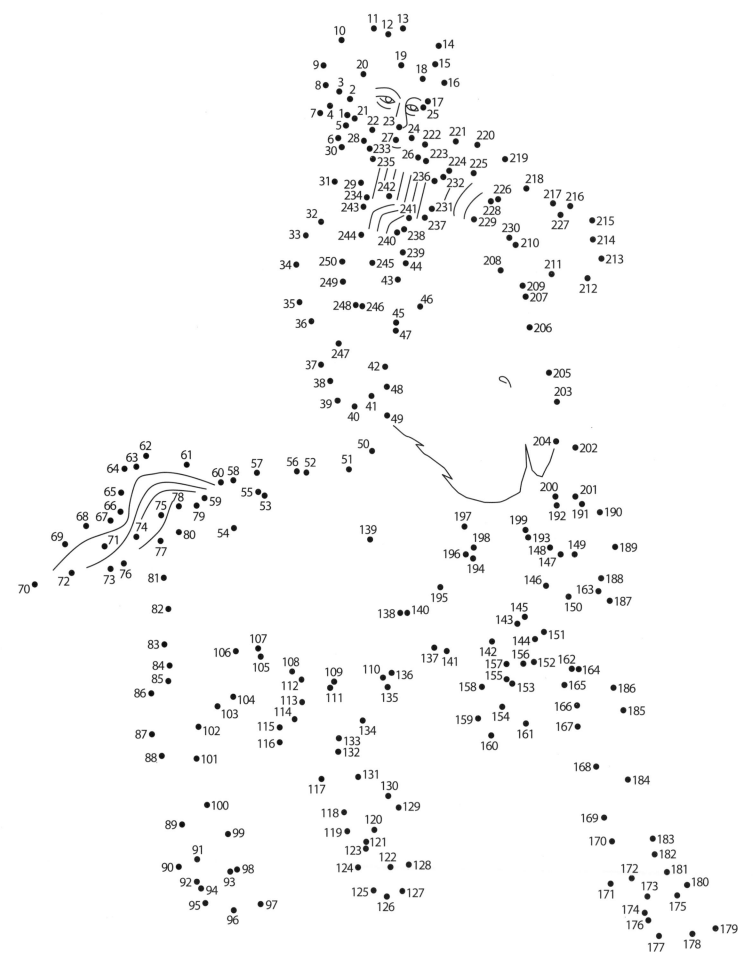

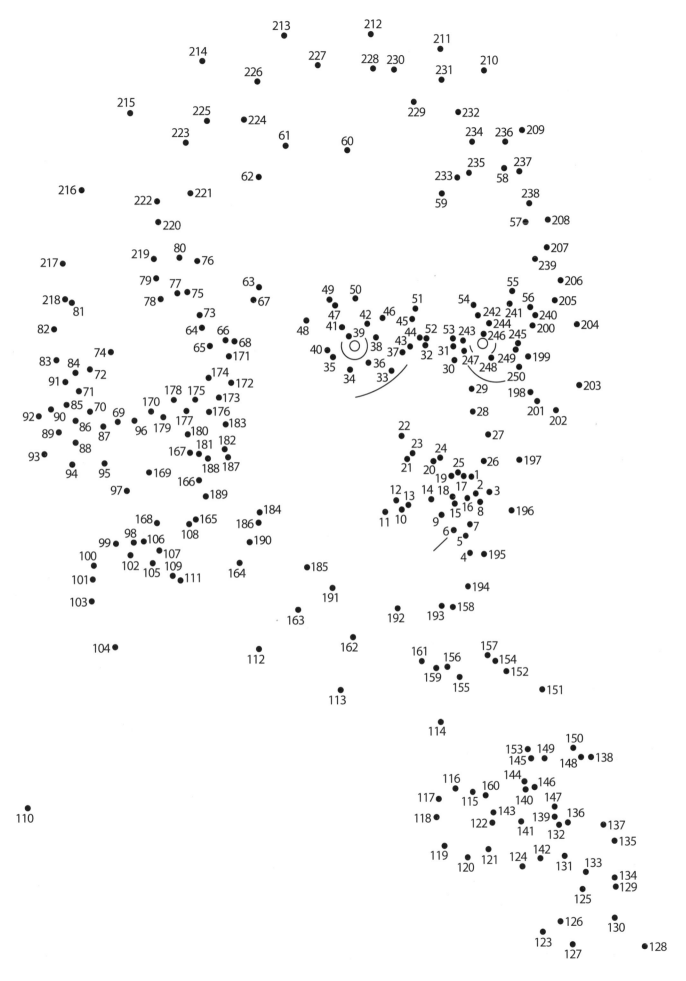

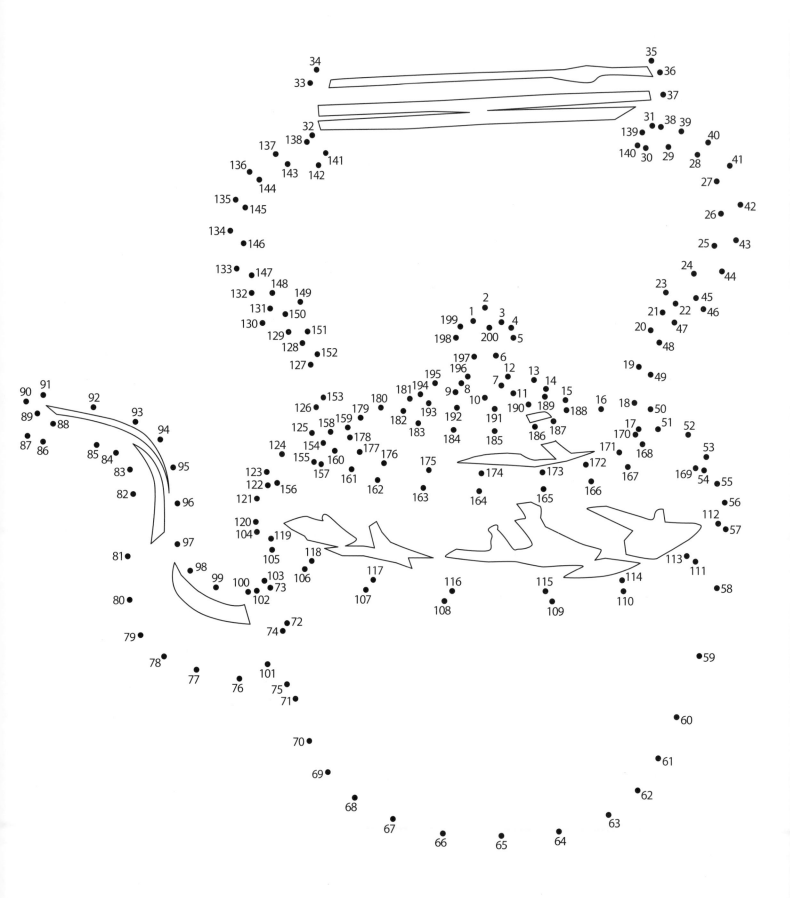

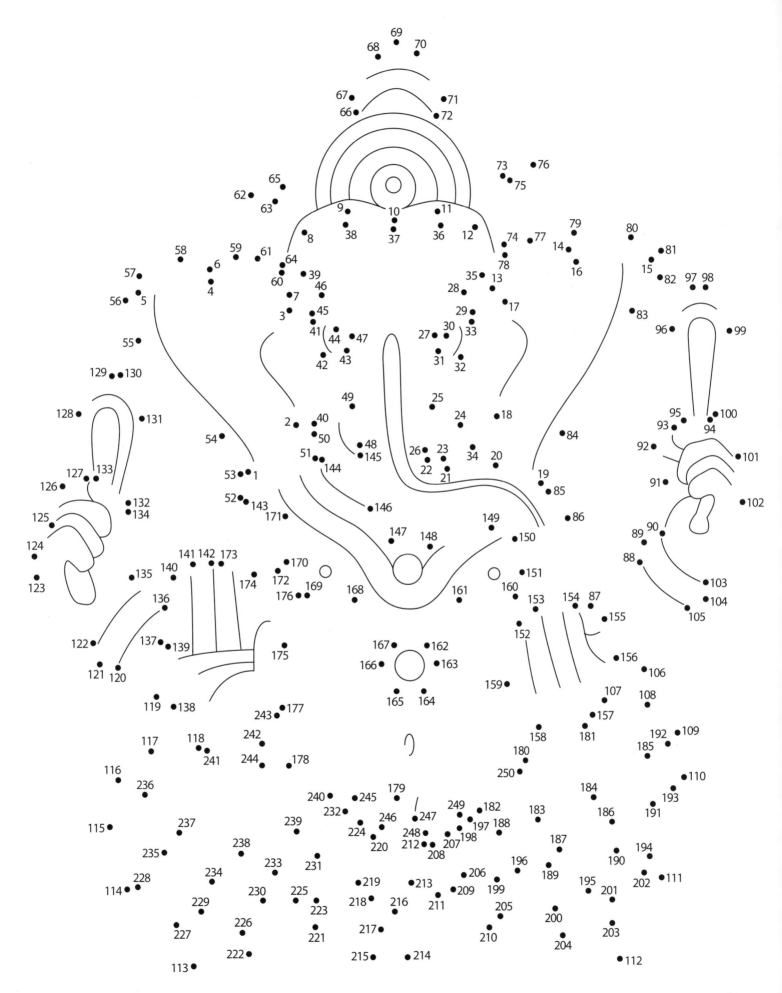

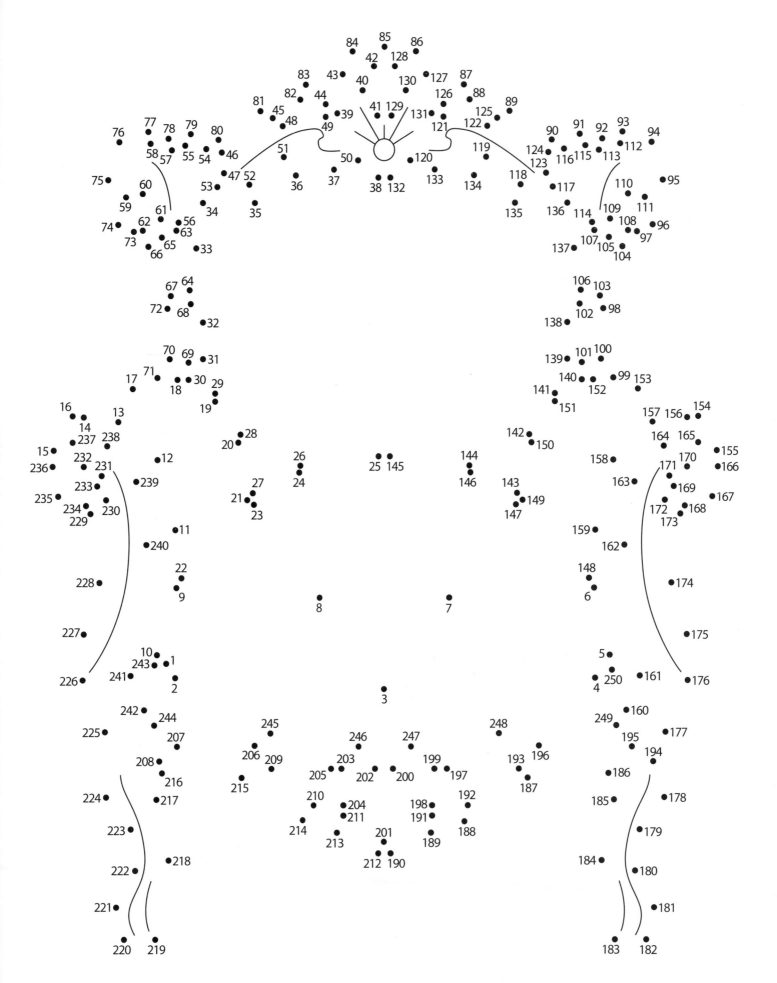

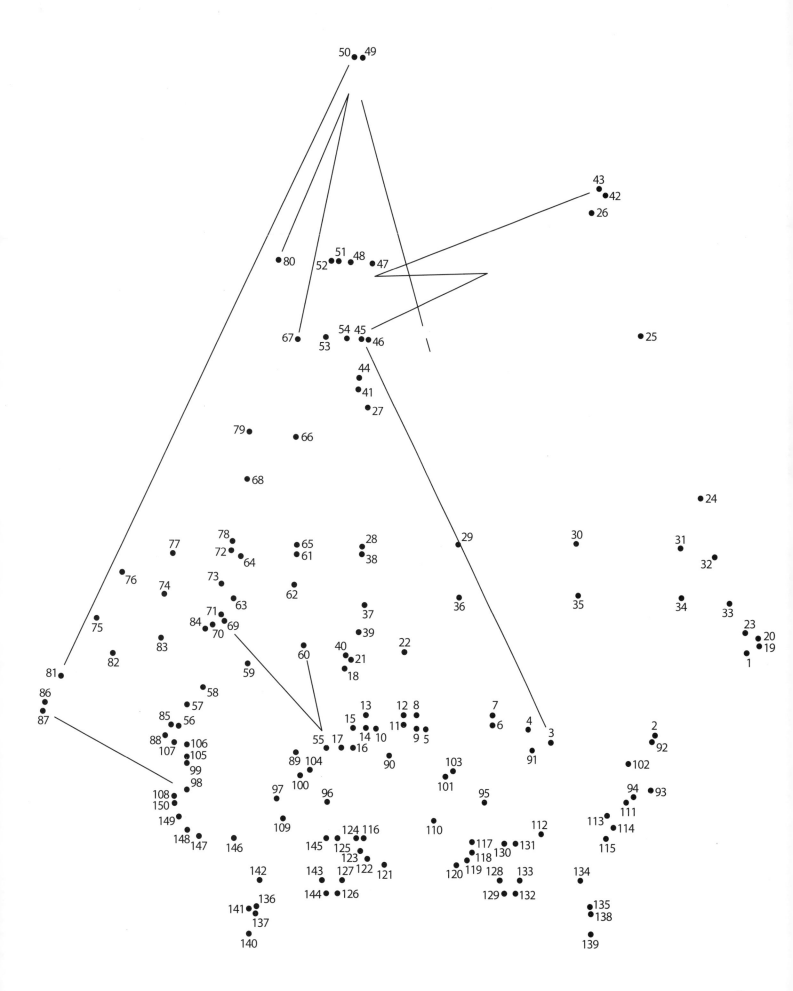

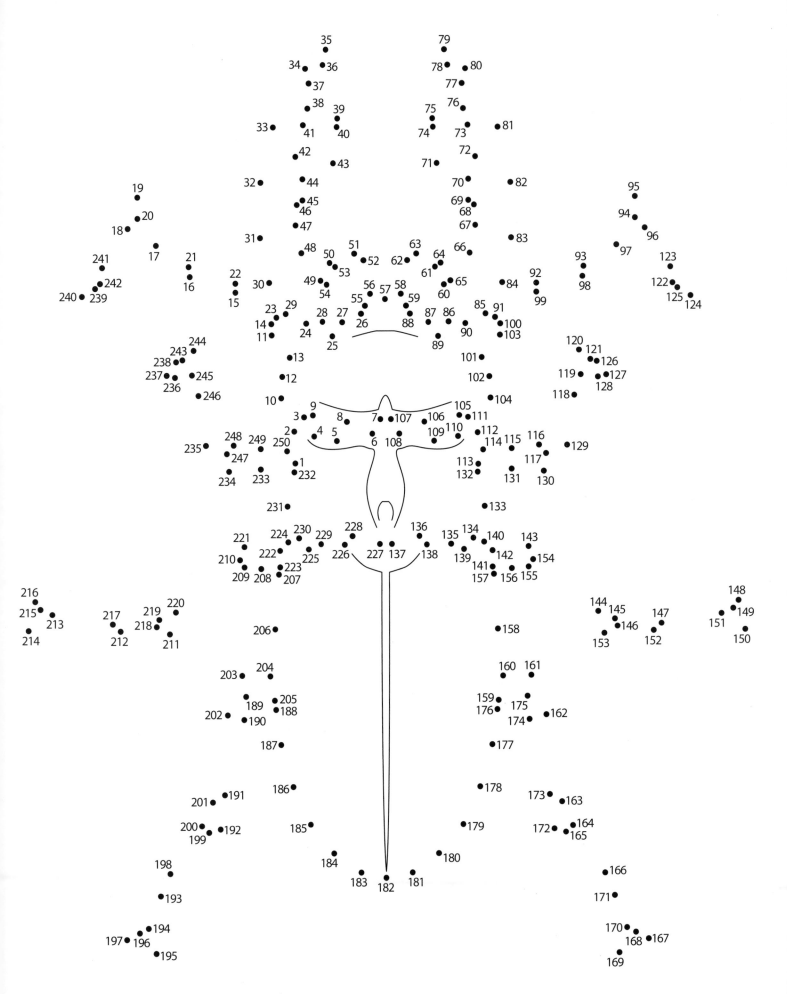

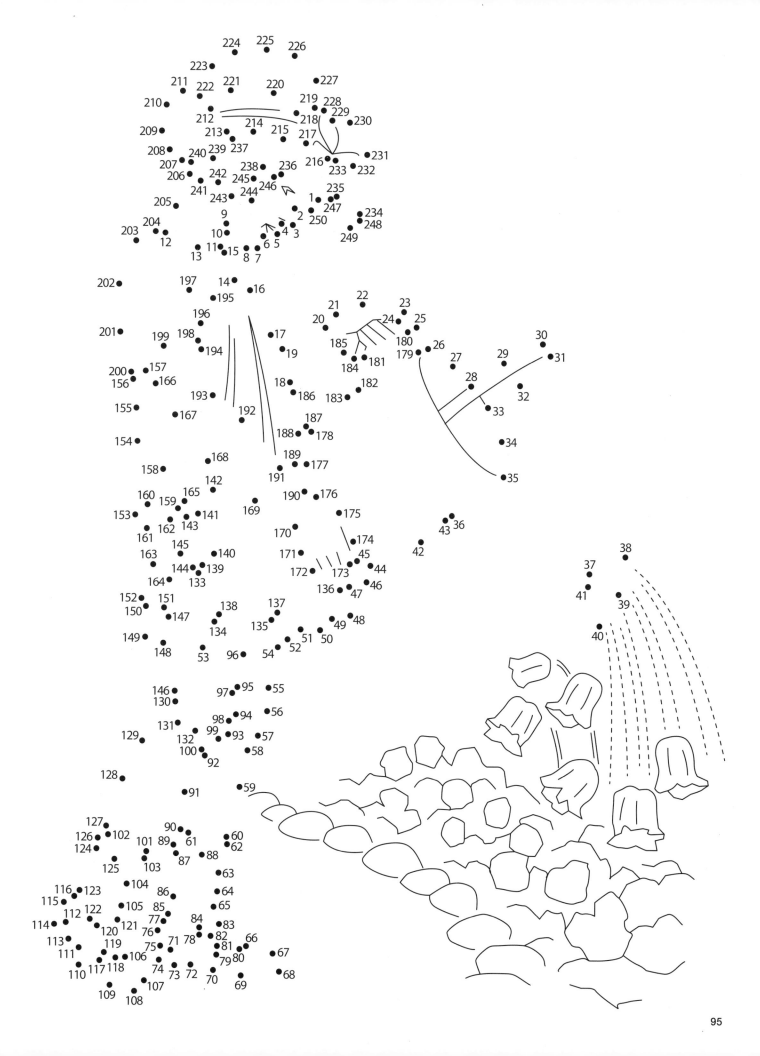

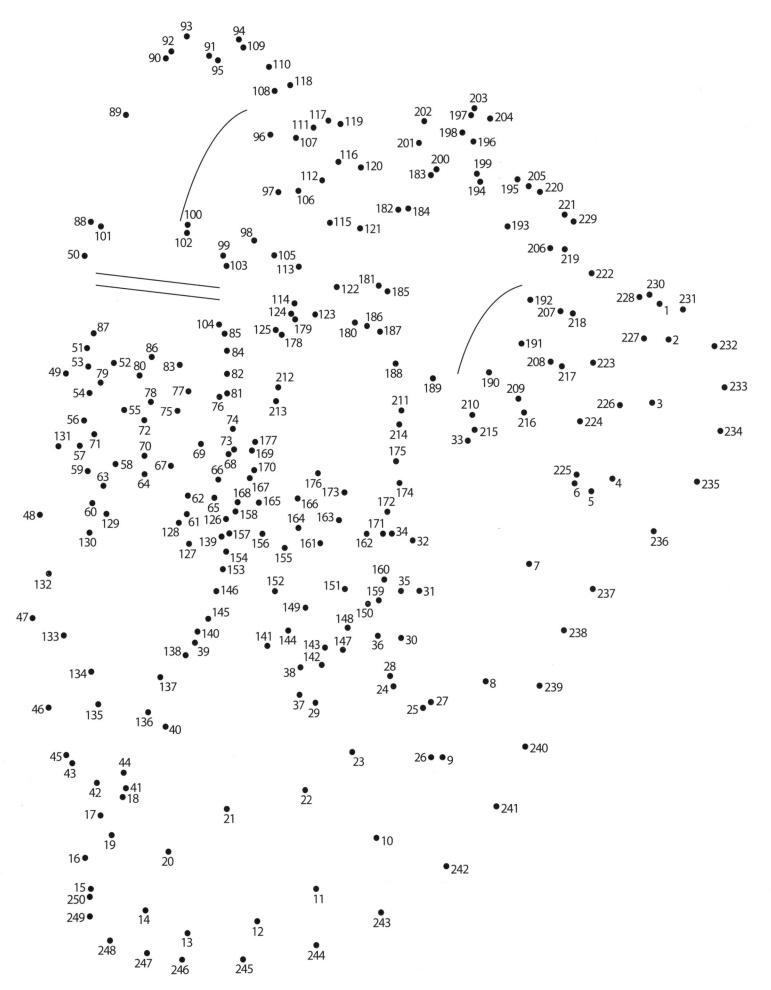

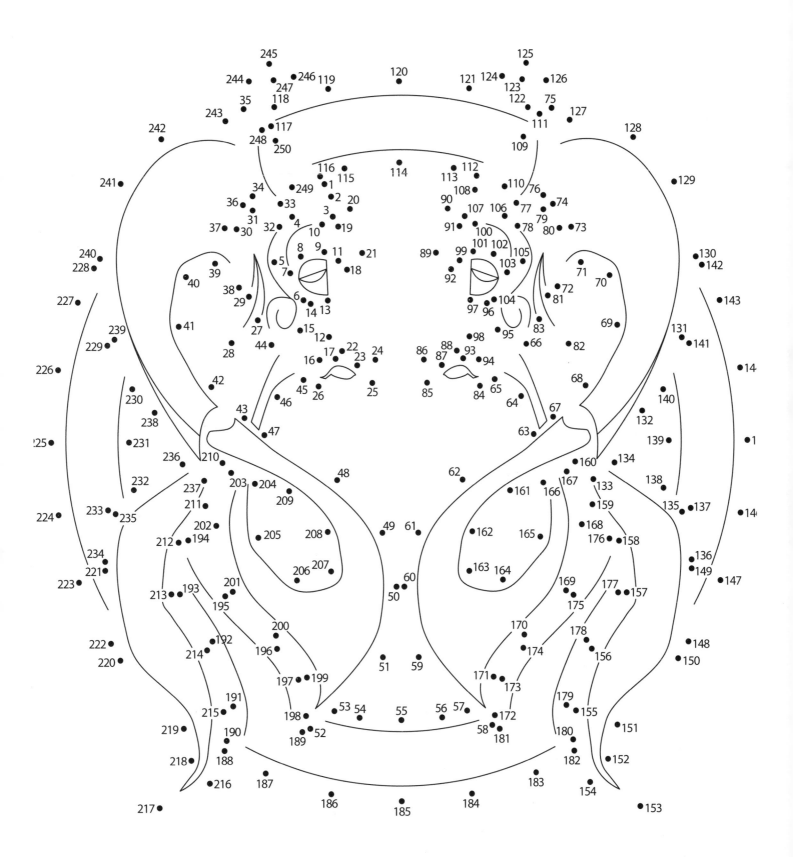

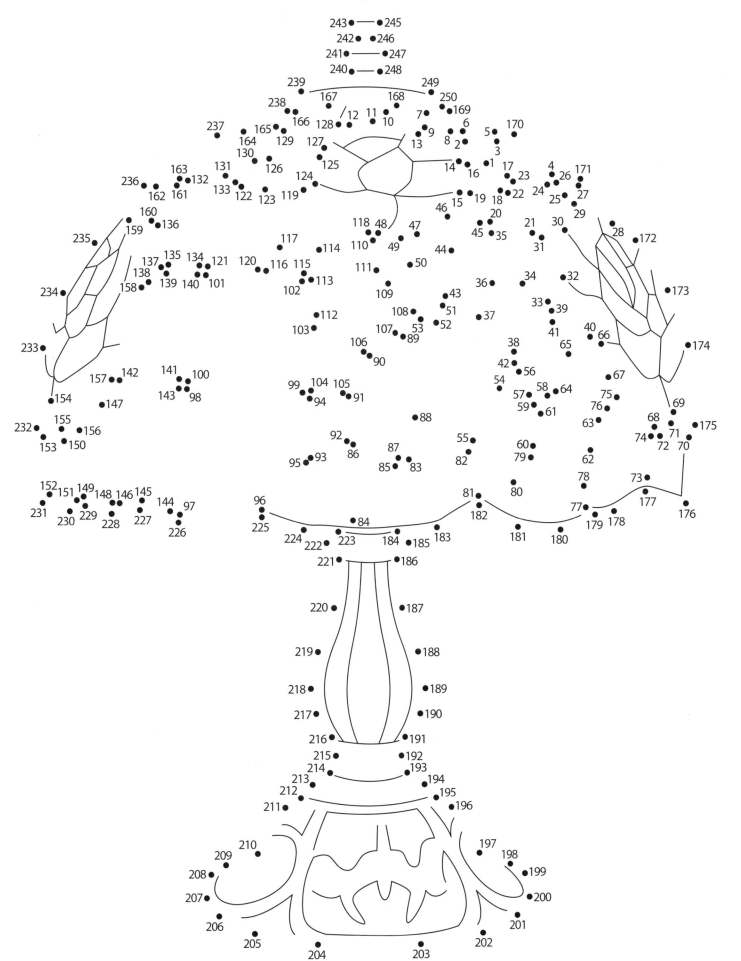

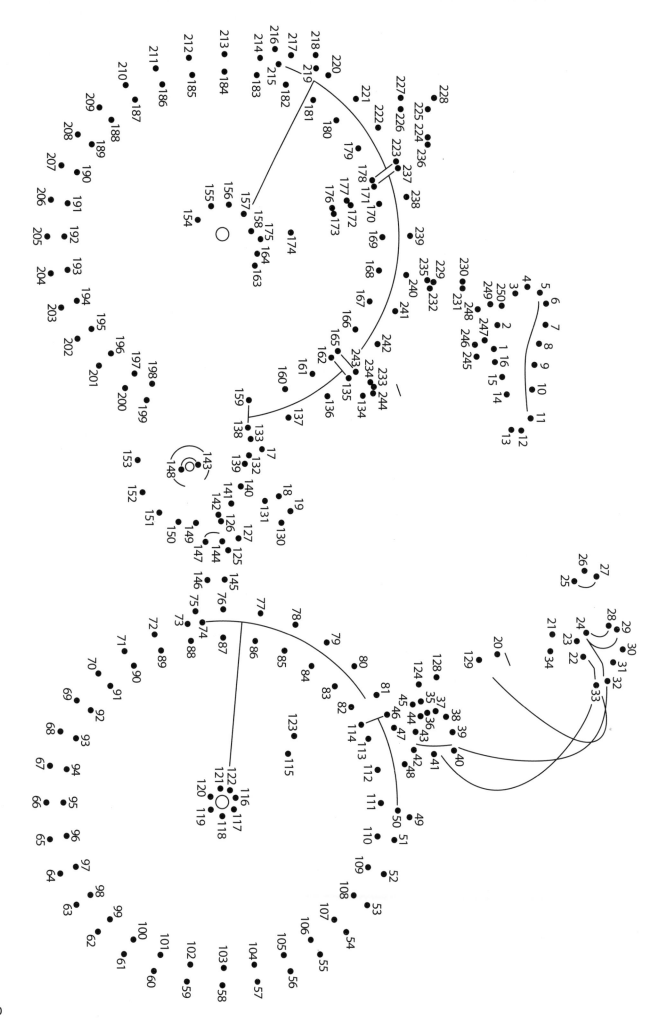

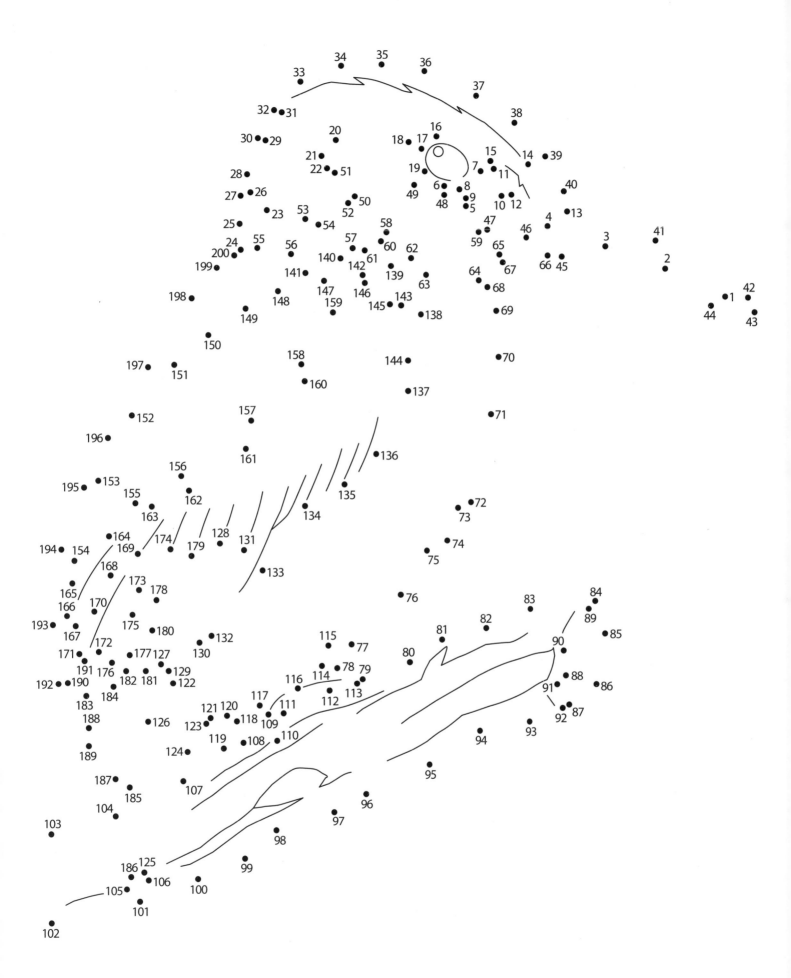

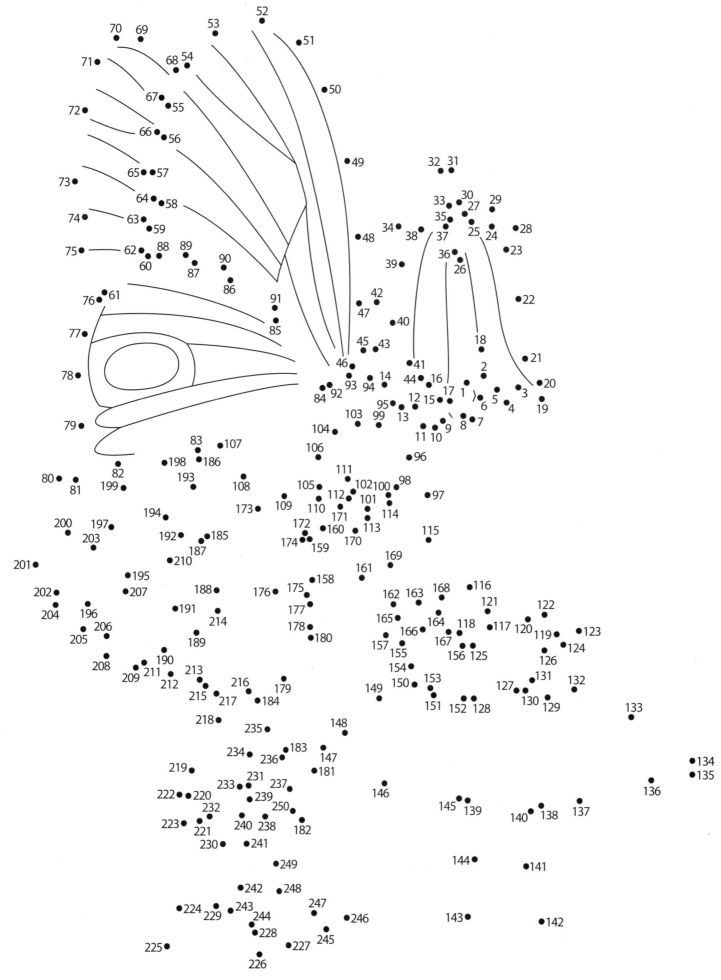

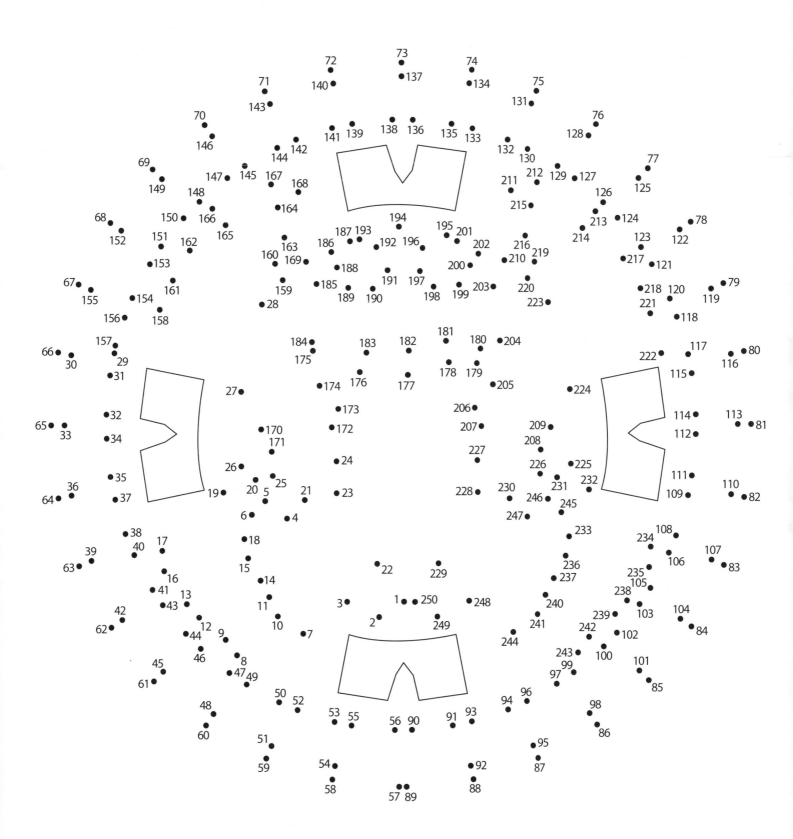

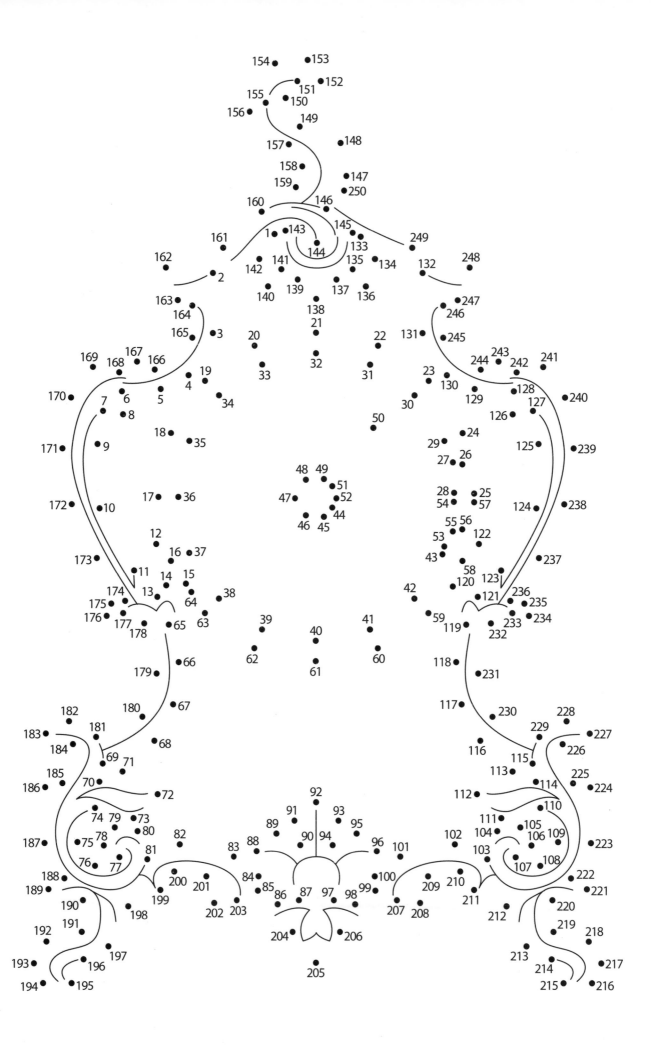

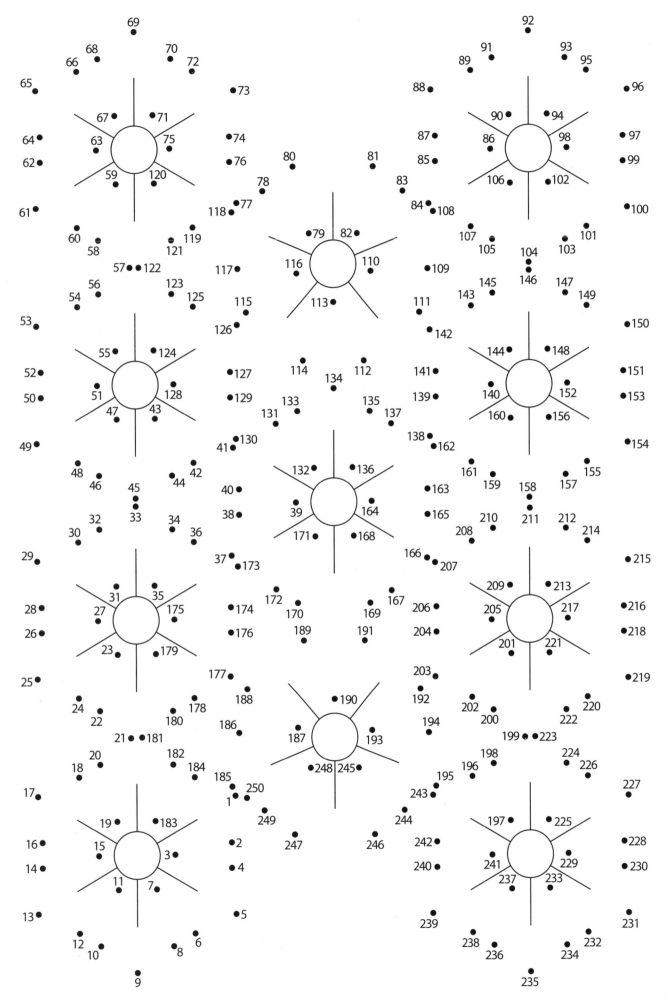

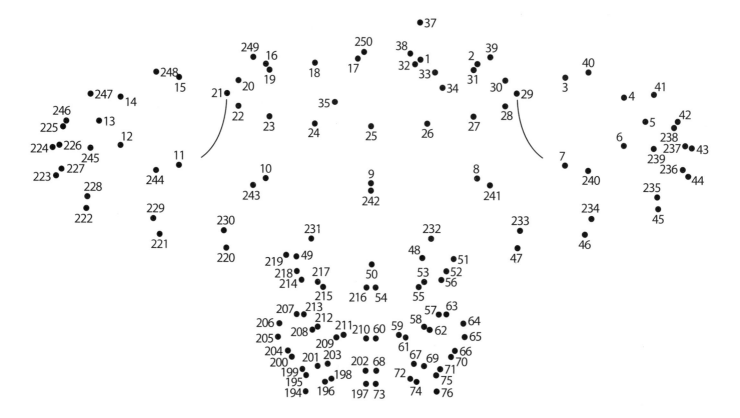

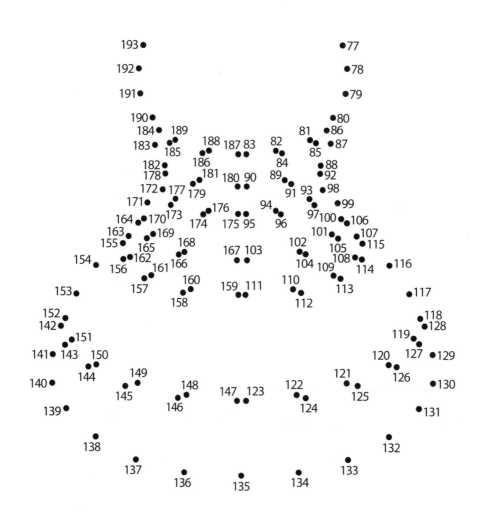

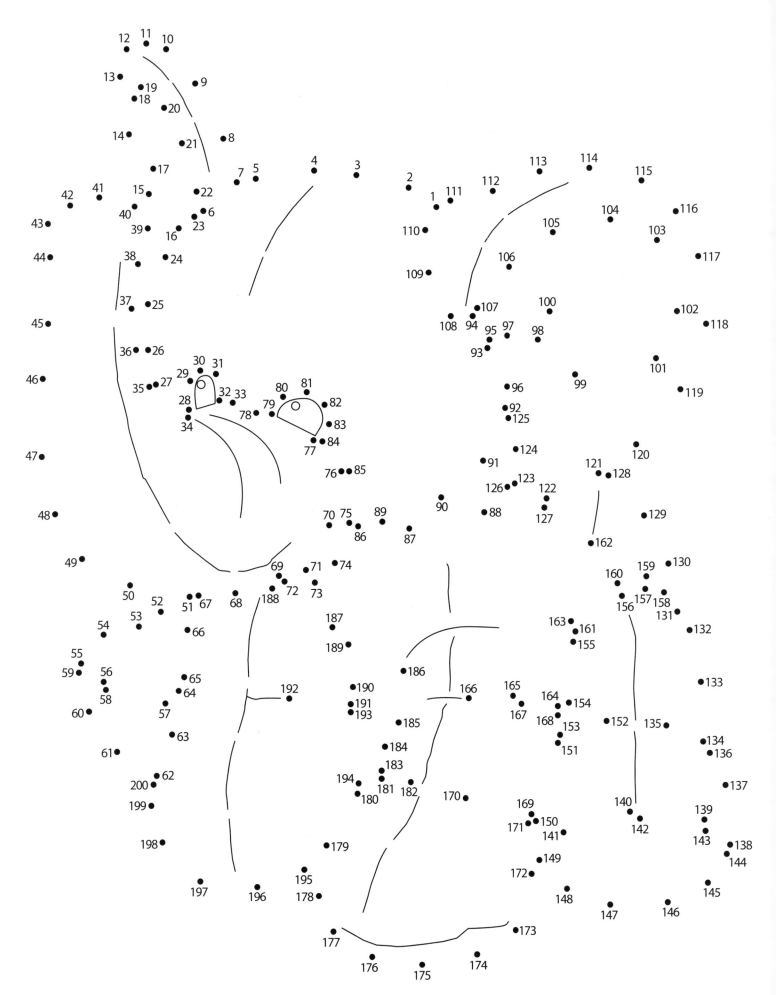

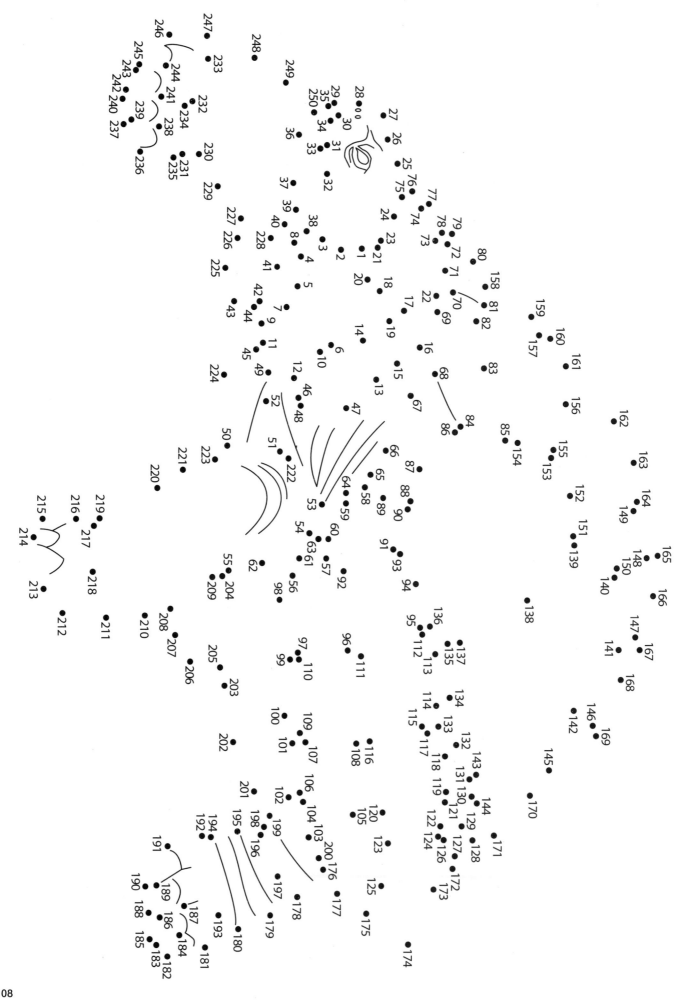

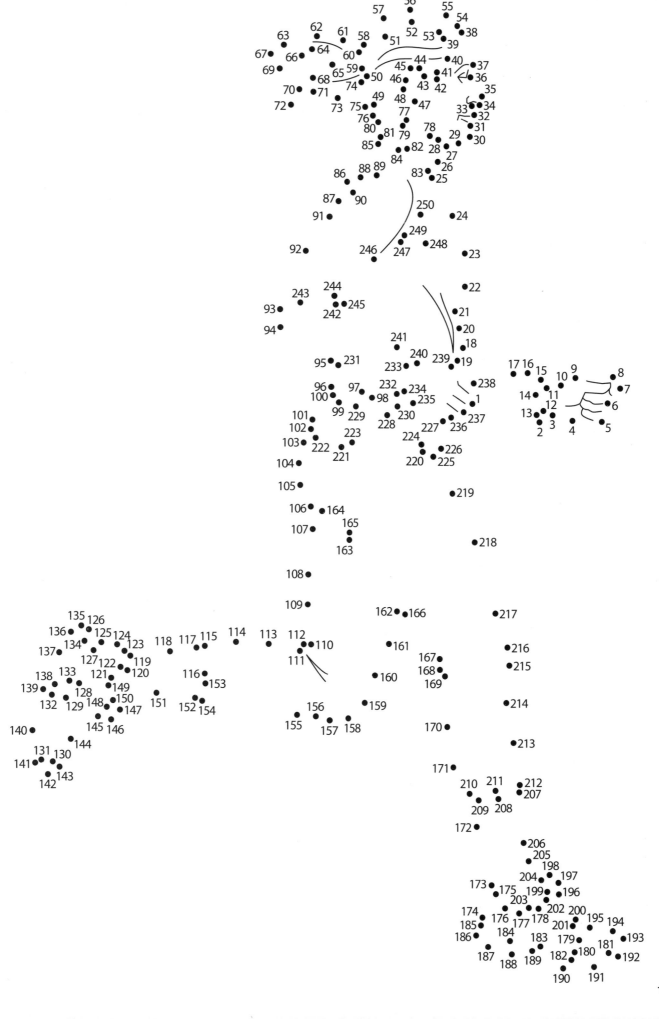

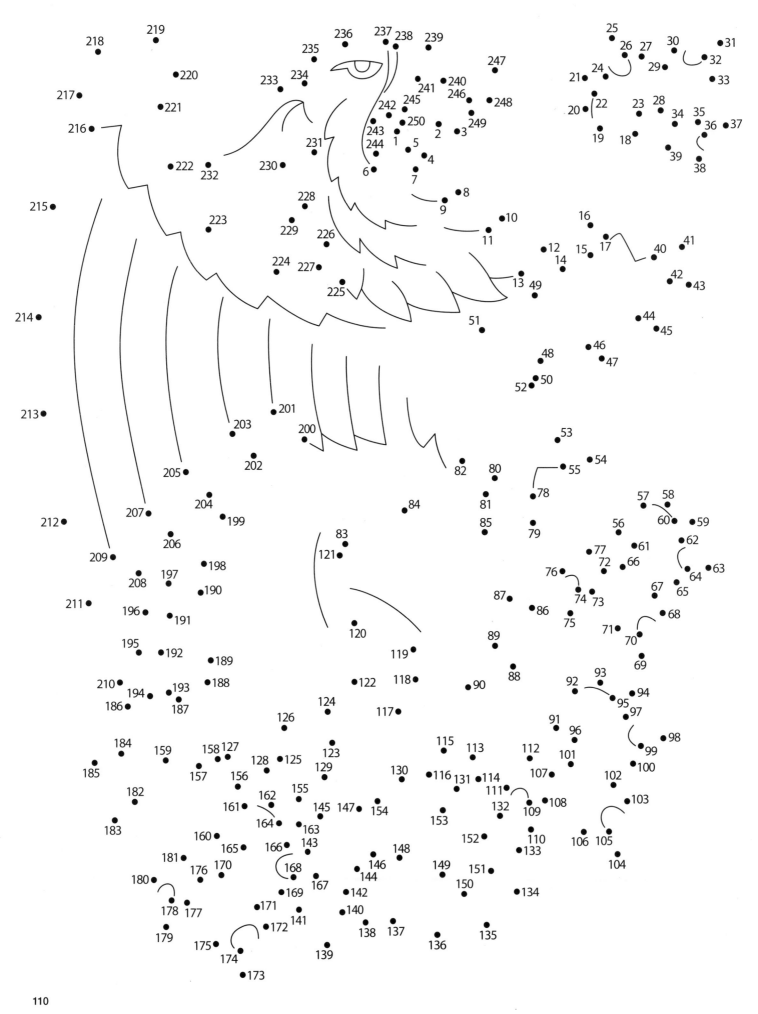

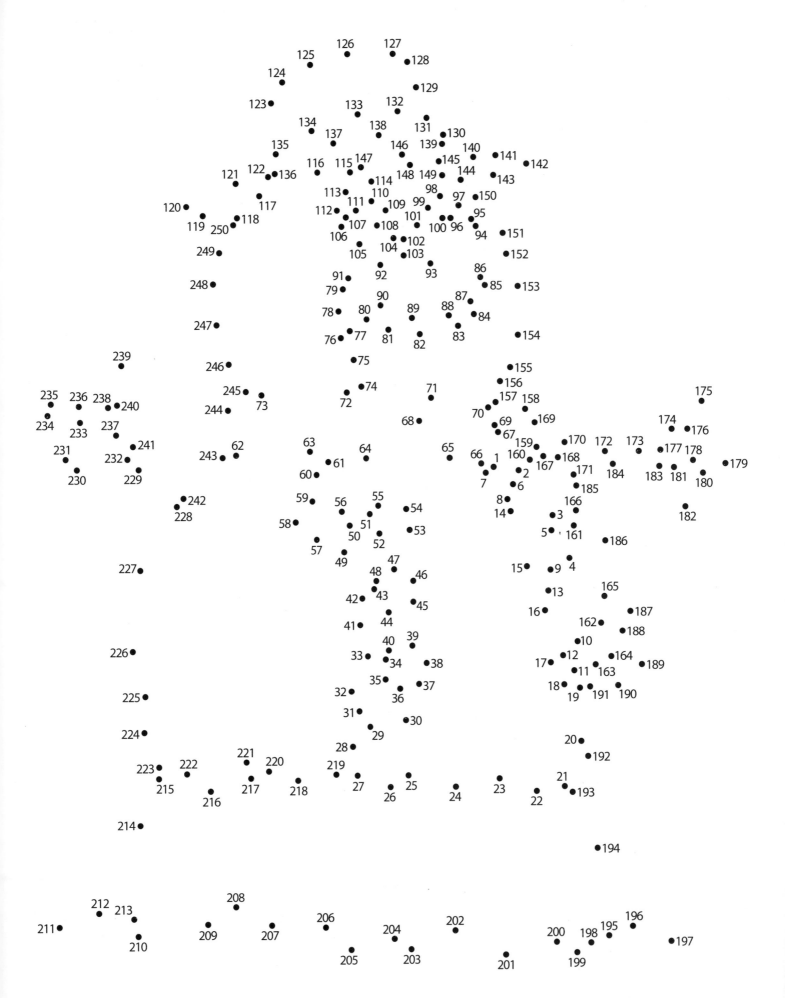

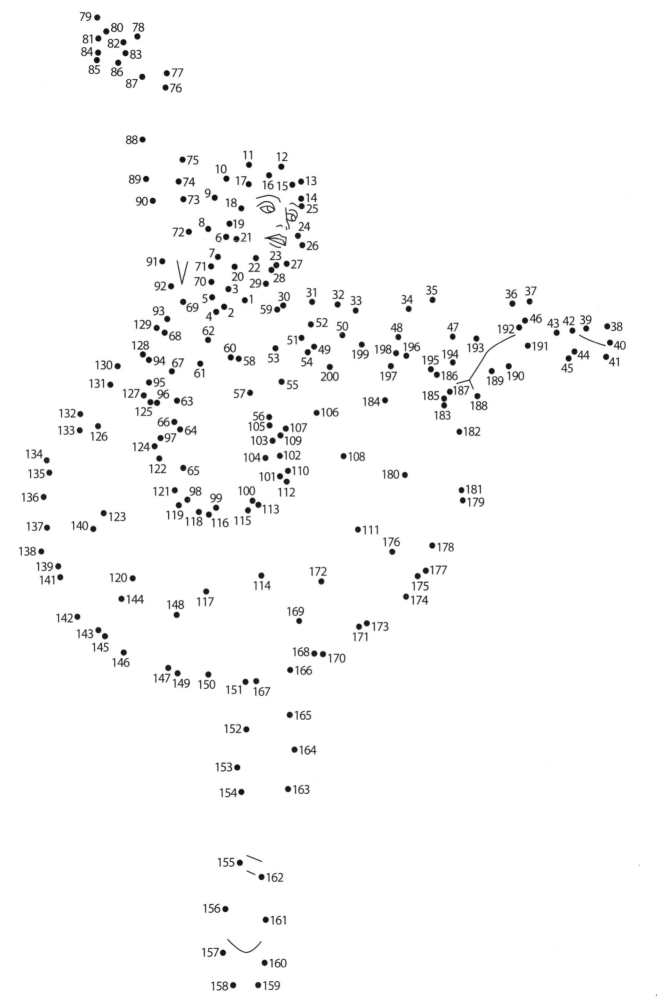

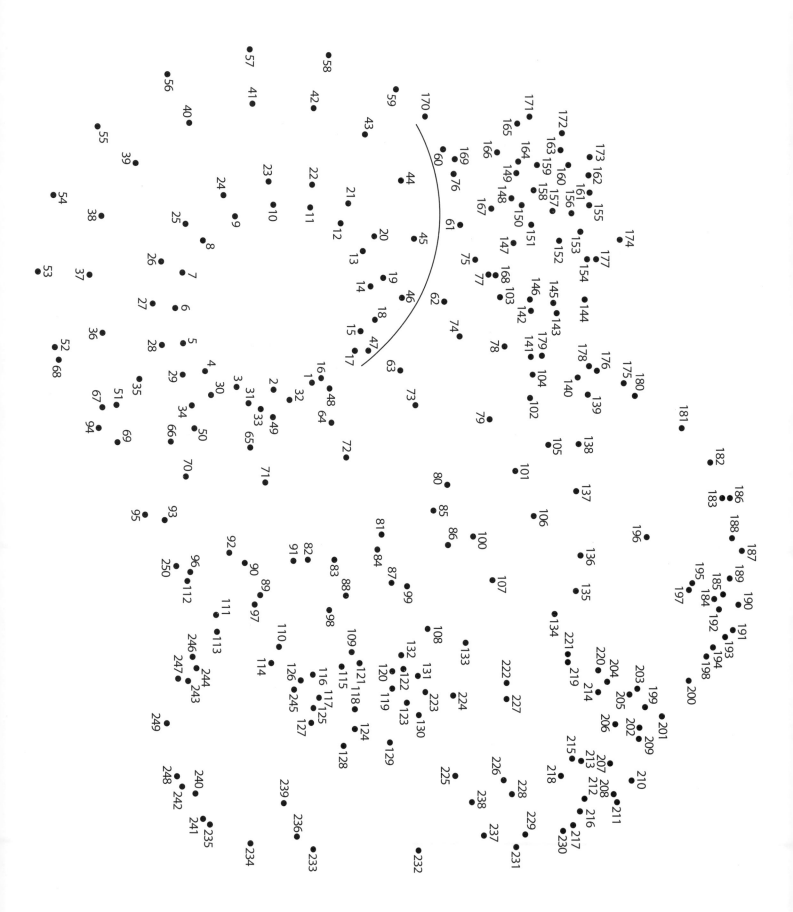

114

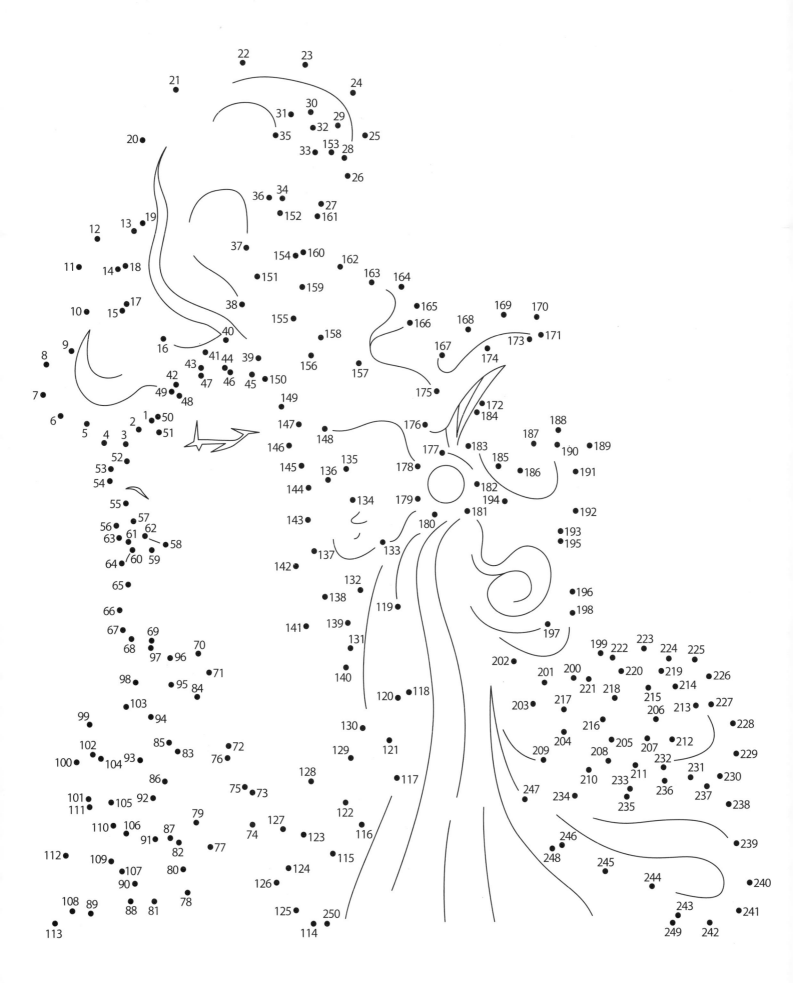

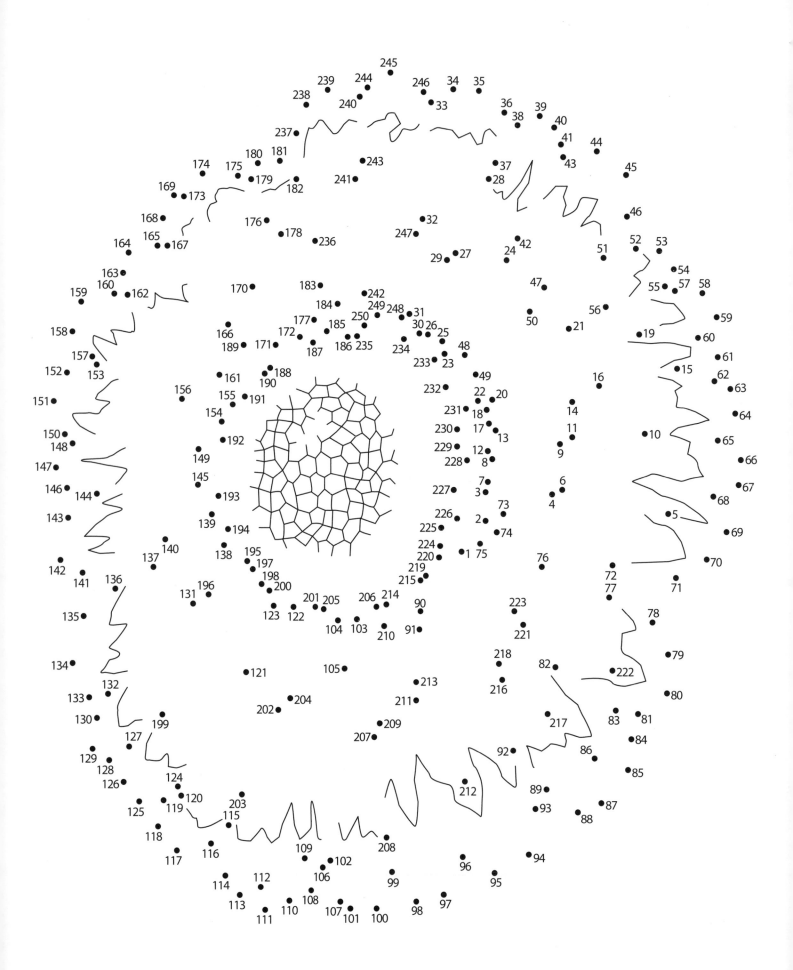

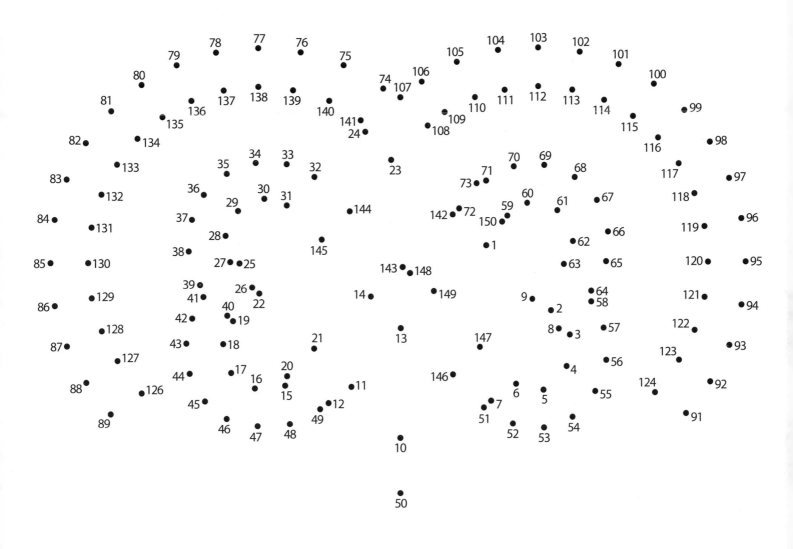

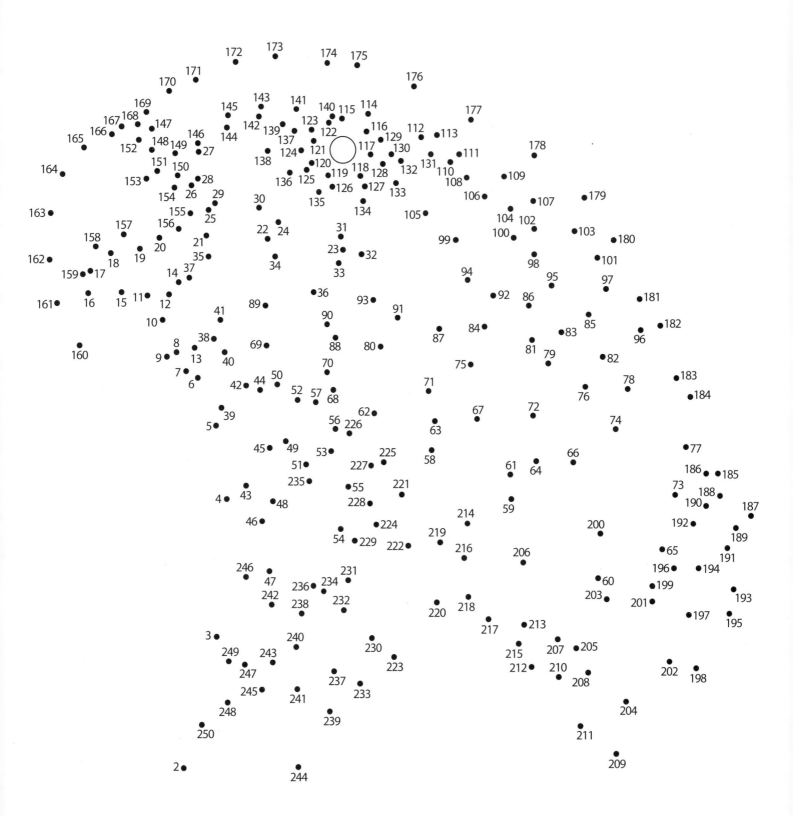

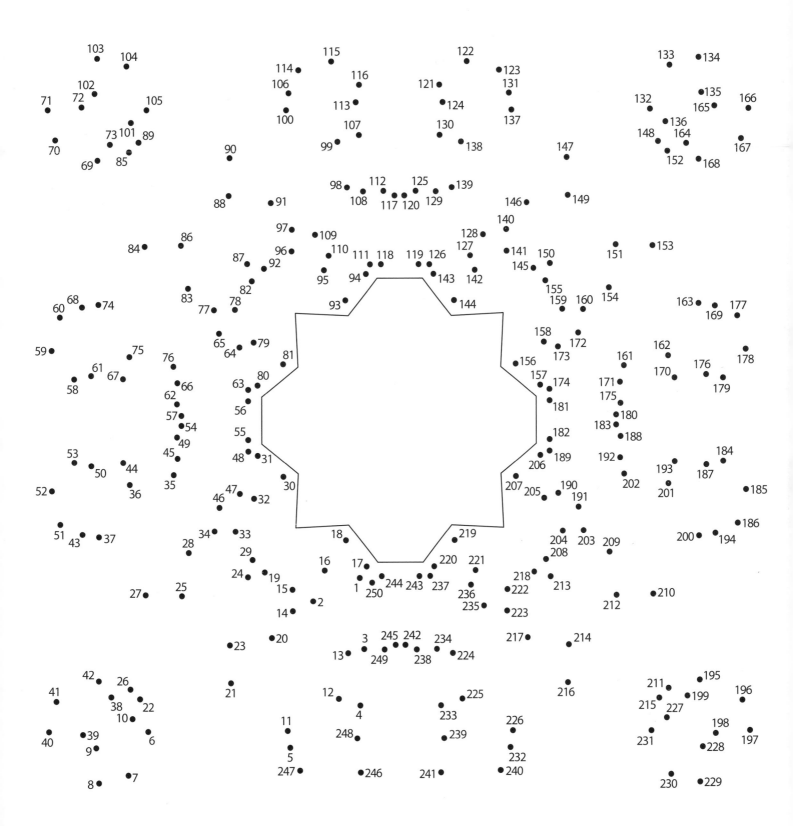

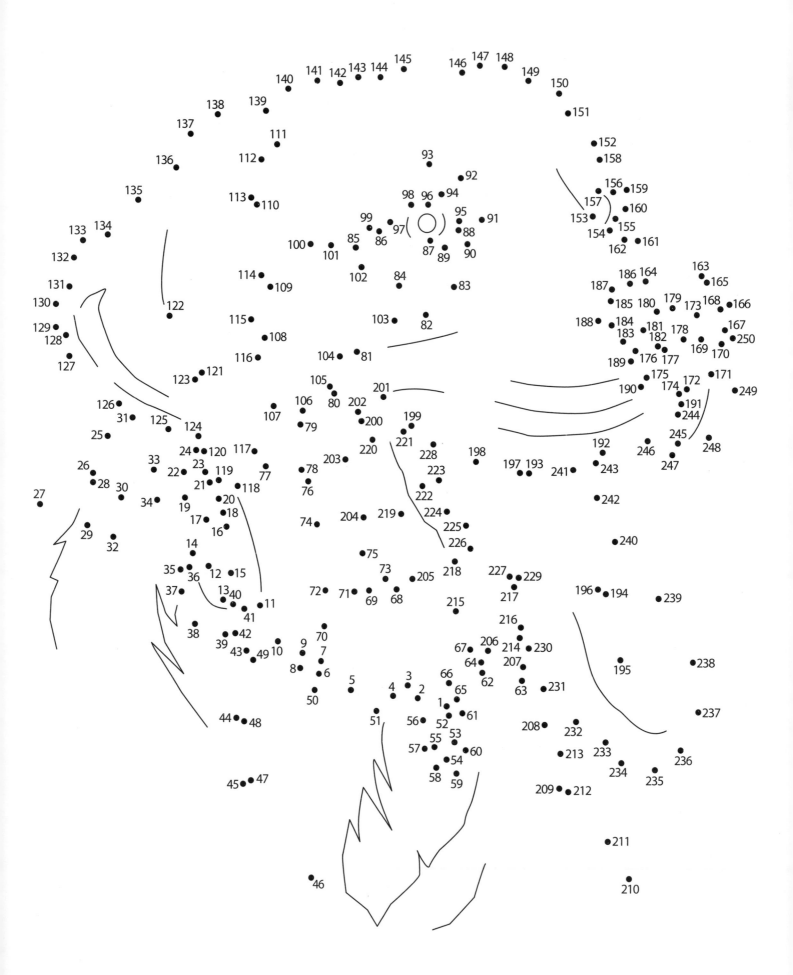

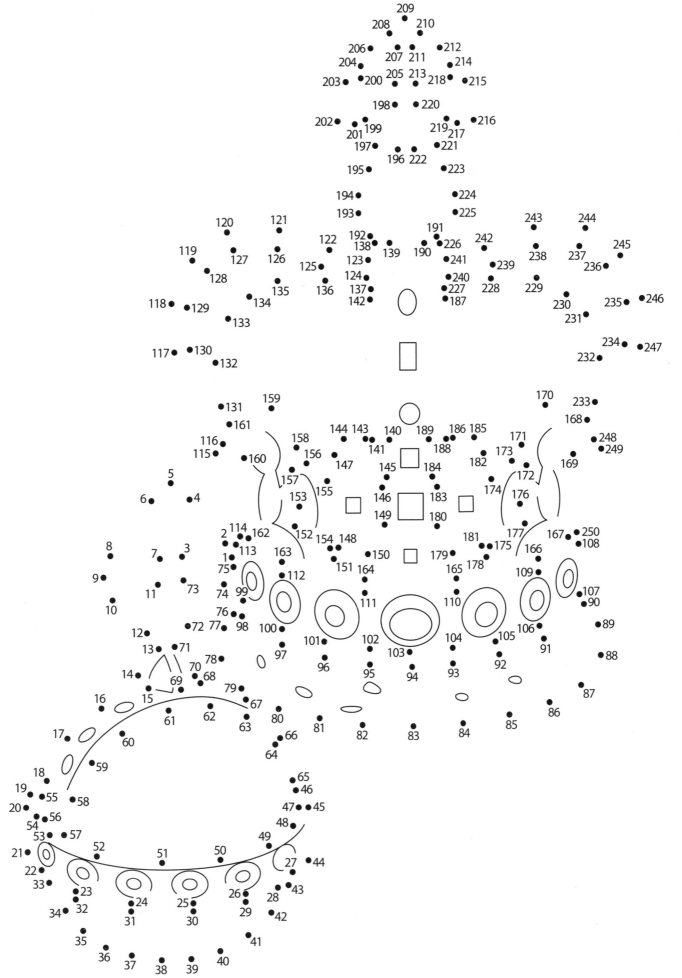

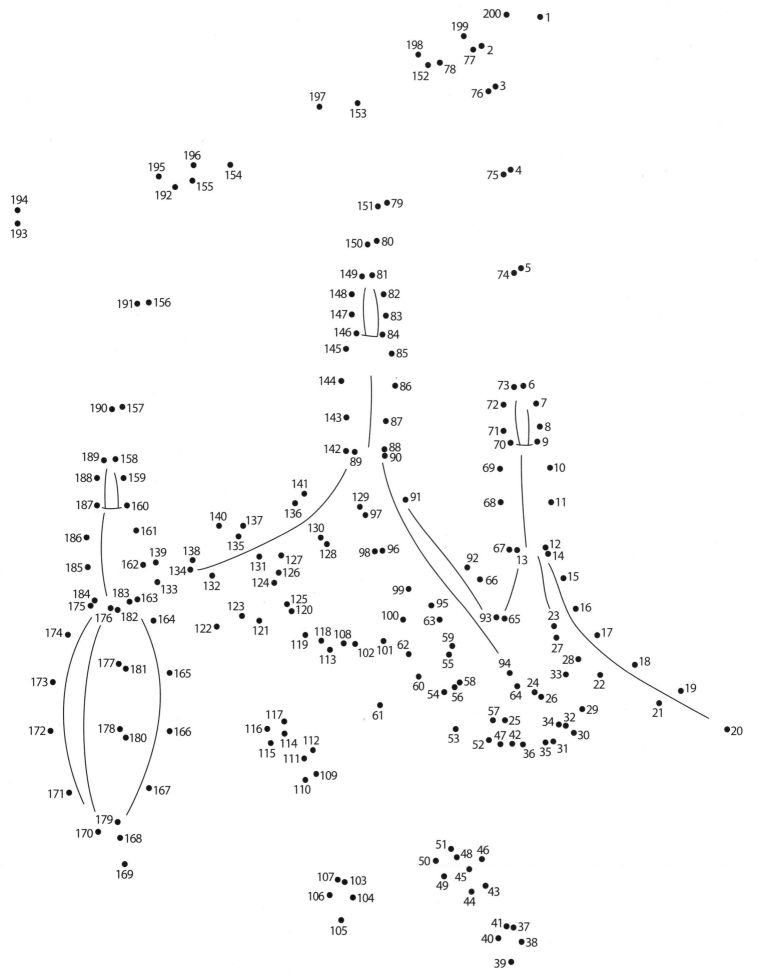

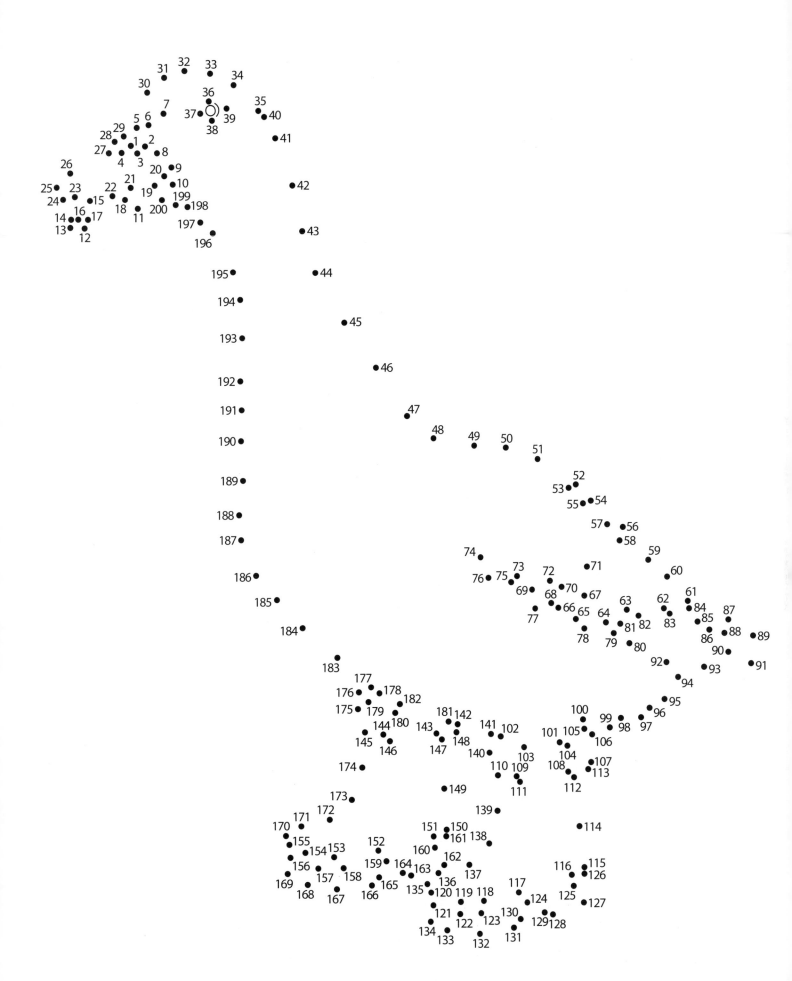

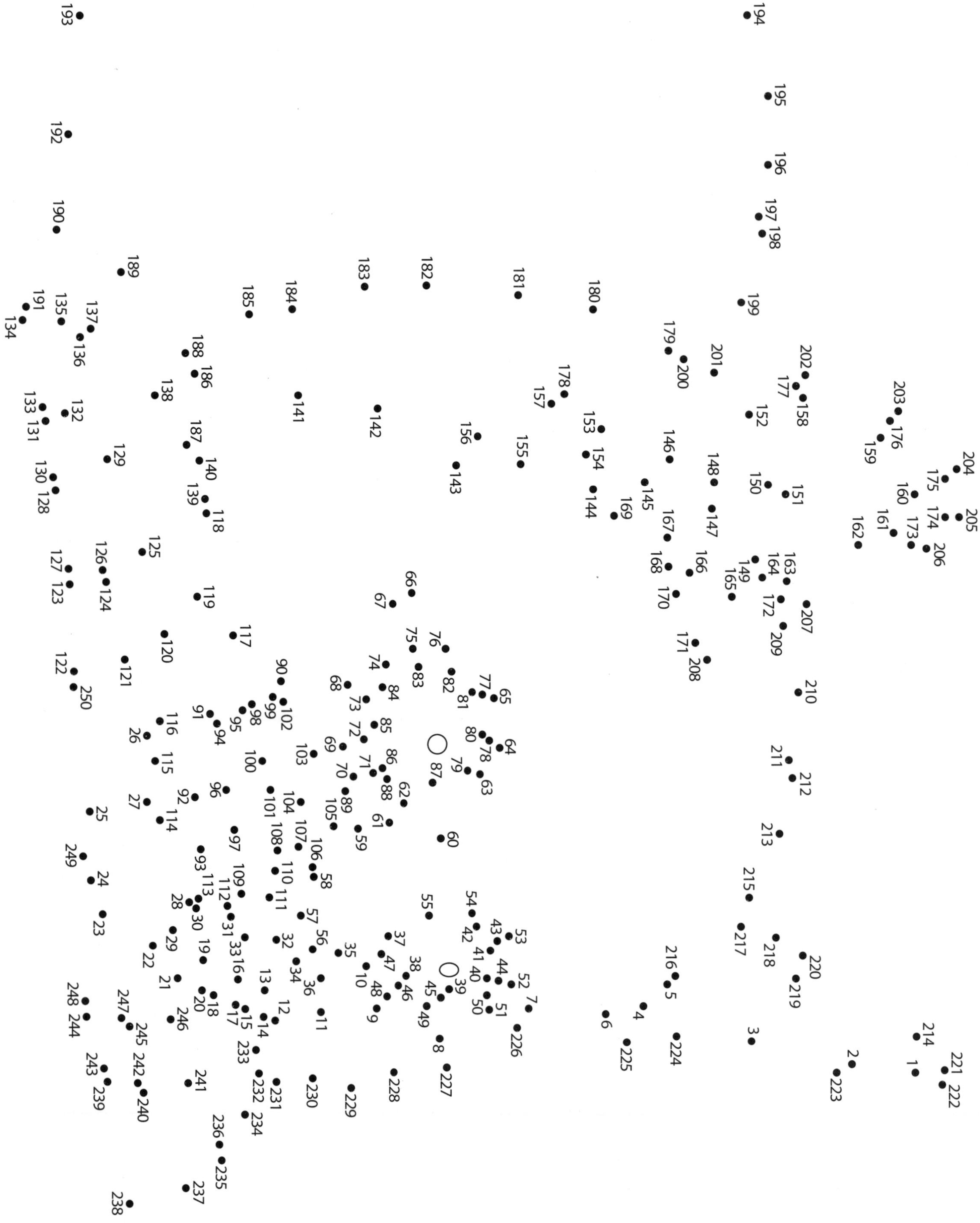

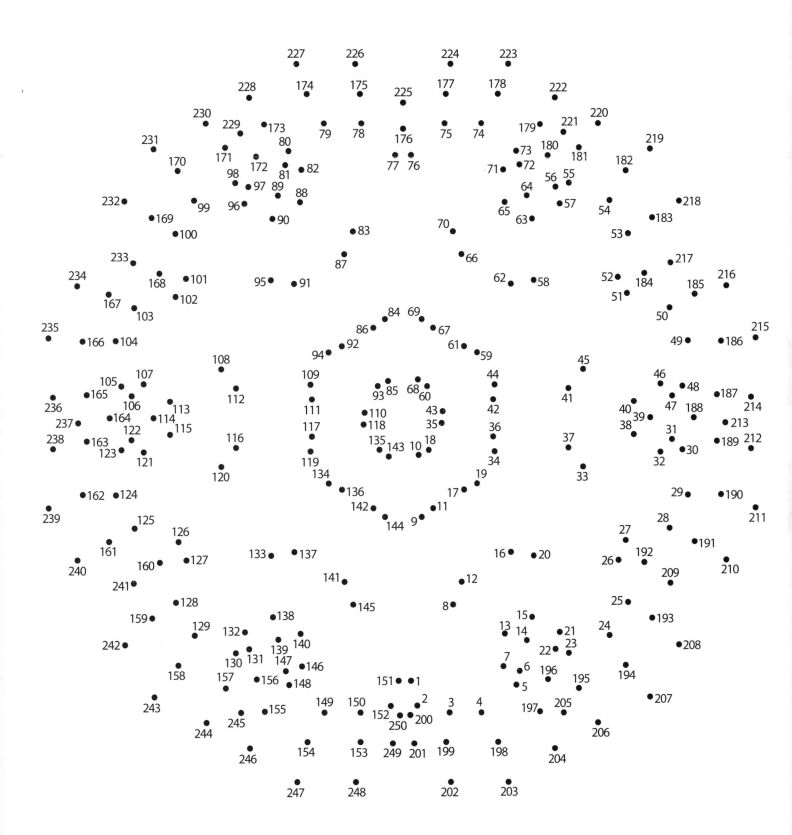

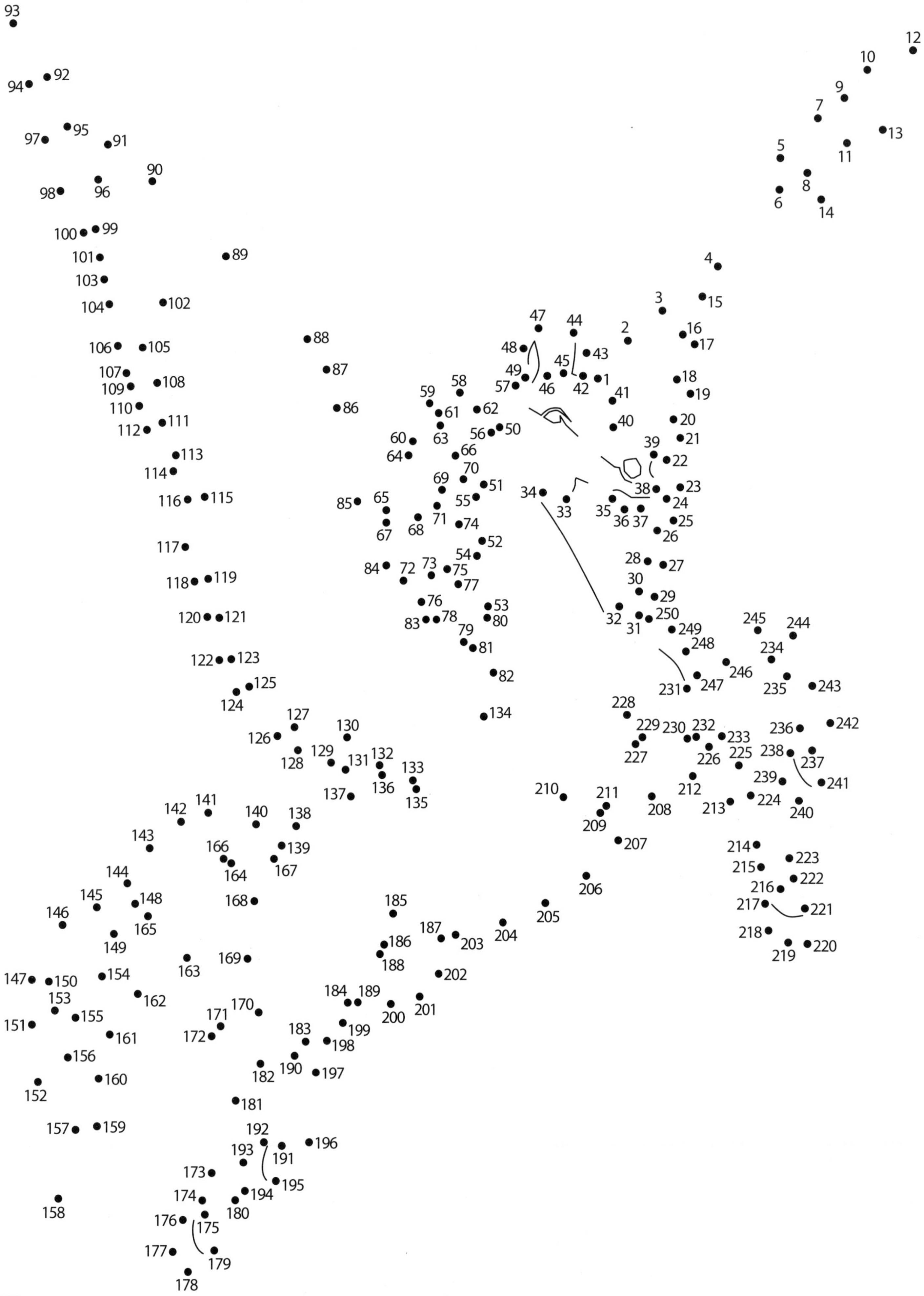

LIST OF ILLUSTRATIONS